At Issue

| Should the US Close
Its Borders?

Other Books in the At Issue Series:

At Issue

Should the US Close Its Borders?

Louise I. Gerdes, Book Editor

GREENHAVEN PRESS
A part of Gale, Cengage Learning

GALE
CENGAGE Learning·

Detroit • New York • San Francisco • New Haven, Conn • Waterville, Maine • London

Elizabeth Des Chenes, *Director, Content Strategy*
Cynthia Sanner, *Publisher*
Douglas Dentino, *Manager, New Product*

For more information, contact:
Greenhaven Press
27500 Drake Rd.
Farmington Hills, MI 48331-3535
Or you can visit our Internet site at www.gale.cengage.com

For product information and technology assistance, contact us at

Gale Customer Support, 1-800-877-4253
For permission to use material from this text or product, submit all requests online at www.cengage.com/permissions.

Further permissions questions can be e-mailed to permissionrequest@cengage.com.

Articles in Greenhaven Press anthologies are often edited for length to meet page requirements. In addition, original titles of these works are changed to clearly present the main thesis and to explicitly indicate the author's opinion. Every effort is made to ensure that Greenhaven Press accurately reflects the original intent of the authors. Every effort has been made to trace the owners of copyrighted material.

Cover photograph copyright © Images.com/Corbis.

LIBRARY OF CONGRESS CATALOGING-IN-PUBLICATION DATA

Should the US close Its borders? / Louise I. Gerdes, book editor.
    p. cm. -- (At issue)
    Summary: "At Issue: Should the US Close Its Borders?: Books in this anthology series focus a wide range of viewpoints onto a single controversial issue, providing in-depth discussions by leading advocates, a quick grounding in the issues, and a challenge to critical thinking skills"-- Provided by publisher.
    Includes bibliographical references and index.
    ISBN 978-0-7377-6860-2 (hardback) -- ISBN 978-0-7377-6861-9 (paperback)
    1. Border security--United States--Juvenile literature. 2. United States--Emigration and immigration--Juvenile literature. 3. National security--Law and legislation--United States--Juvenile literature. I. Gerdes, Louise I., 1953-
    JV6483.S554 2014
    363.28'50973--dc23
                                                        2013035191

Printed in the United States of America
1 2 3 4 5 6 7 18 17 16 15 14

Contents

Introduction

America is a nation built by immigrants, and for most of its history the United States has generally opened its borders to those seeking a better way of life. However, Americans have also been of two minds about immigration. Journalist and Supreme Court analyst Kenneth Jost writes, "Immigrants are alternately celebrated as the source of diversity and criticized as agents of disunity. Immigrants were recruited to till the soil, build the cities and labor in the factories, but often criticized for taking jobs from and lowering wages for the citizen workforce."[1] Public concern about immigration has fluctuated over the years. In times of economic prosperity, most Americans welcome immigrants. In times of economic insecurity, however, when native-born citizens must compete with immigrants for scarce resources, attitudes toward immigration often turn negative. Opposition also grows when Americans feel their security is threatened. In an effort to address the ebb and flow of public opinion, policy makers establish immigration policies that attempt to balance the benefits and challenges of immigration. These often conflicting goals also reflect the contentious nature of the border debate.

During the nation's first two hundred years, US borders remained mostly open to immigrants. Americans, many of whom were themselves immigrants or the children of immigrants, generally valued the economic and cultural benefits of immigration, although policy makers did, at times, establish restrictions and limits. The 1921 Emergency Quota Act and the 1924 Johnson-Reed Act instituted quotas that favored immigrants from northern Europe over those from southern Europe and elsewhere. However, the Immigration and Nationality Act of 1965 abolished the quota system. Drafted during the

---

1. Kenneth Jost, "Immigration Conflict," *CQ Researcher*, March 9, 2012.

civil rights movement, the act reflected the belief that quotas based on national origins ran contrary to American values. Thus, the act favored the reunification of families and encouraged the immigration of those who could contribute to the nation's workforce, regardless of their origins. However, the demographics of immigration from the late 1960s to the late 1970s changed. According to the *INS Statistical Yearbook,* by 1978 44 percent of legal immigration came from the Americas and 42 percent from Asia. Only 12 percent came from Europe during these years. Moreover, the flow of illegal immigration also increased, particularly at the nation's southern border.

In the mid-1980s, Census Bureau estimates indicated that as many as three to five million undocumented immigrants lived in the United States. This dramatic increase changed attitudes toward immigration among some Americans. Polls taken during the period revealed that as many as two-thirds of Americans wanted to decrease immigration and stem the flow across US borders. Some feared illegal immigrants were taking jobs from Americans, using taxpayer-funded benefits, and contributing to an increase in crime. Those who supported more open borders argued that immigrants strengthen the economy and provide more stable communities, because most immigrants are highly invested in the nation and are less prone to crime. These conflicting views made immigration an extremely contentious issue during the 1980s. In response, at that time and in the decades that followed, policy makers tried a variety of different strategies to control legal and illegal immigration.

During the 1980s, the primary public concern about America's borders was the flow of immigrants entering the nation illegally. Policy makers responded with the Immigration Reform and Control Act of 1986. The law attempted to reduce the flow of illegal immigration while meeting the continuing need for immigrant labor. The act granted amnesty for undocumented immigrants who had been in the country since 1982. However, to deter illegal immigration, the act made employing undocumented workers illegal. Civil rights organizations feared that the law would increase discrimination against Latino citizens seeking work. In truth, the enforcement of these provisions proved challenging. Indeed, the law failed to ease concerns among many about the impact of illegal immigration.

During the 1990s, new strategies emerged to stem the flow of illegal immigrants crossing US borders. A grassroots movement in California hoped to deter illegal immigration by denying government benefits such as health care and education to those who could not prove citizenship. Although California's hotly contested Proposition 187 passed, the state never enforced the law. A 1982 Supreme Court ruling found unconstitutional any laws that denied school-age alien children an education. Moreover, Latino voters helped elect a Democratic governor who did not defend the proposition in the state's court. The federal response in the 1990s took a different direction, focusing on strengthening enforcement, better securing the border, and streamlining deportation policies. The 1996 Illegal Immigration Reform and Immigrant Responsibility Act created an E-Verify system for employers to check the immigration status of its workers and applicants electronically. Although the law appeared strict, the reality proved less so. In truth, deportation proceedings remained backlogged and the E-Verify system was both optional and unreliable. Illegal immigration continued to increase.

The immigration strategy in the early years of the new millennium differed dramatically. In the first eighteen months of his presidency, George W. Bush and leadership in both parties encouraged Congress to pass legislation that would reform immigration laws to encourage Mexican immigration to the United States, arguing that reform would economically benefit both nations. In fact, the economy had improved significantly in the 1990s, and the time seemed ripe to return to policies that opened US borders to immigration. However, all hope of success for this legislation vanished on September 11, 2001, when al Qaeda terrorists attacked the nation, killing thousands. National security became the primary concern, and people questioned immigration policies that allowed al Qaeda terrorists to cross US borders and attack America. Within forty-five days, Congress passed the USA Patriot Act, which among other national security provisions gave the Immigration and Nationalization Service (INS) greater authority to exclude or detain foreigners. The agency was also renamed the US Citizenship and Immigration Service (CIS) and became part of the Department of Homeland Security. Arguably, the 9/11 terrorist attack led to a peak in the number of those who believed America's borders should be closed to immigrants. Nevertheless, despite fears and the efforts to secure America's borders, illegal immigration continued to grow, reaching a high of 12.5 million in 2007, according to the Center for Immigration Studies.

Strategies to balance the costs and benefits of immigration during the second term of Bush's presidency reflect the divisive political climate that created congressional gridlock on many issues, including immigration. The House in 2005 passed a measure that emphasized enforcement—the Border Protection, Antiterrorism, and Illegal Immigration Control Act. The Senate, on the other hand, passed an act that created a path to citizenship for illegal immigrants who had over the years earned the right to citizenship—the Comprehensive Immigration Reform Act of 2006. Neither branch of Congress could agree on much in either bill and neither became law. This gridlock did, however, inspire some state lawmakers to action.

Indeed, some frustrated state lawmakers passed laws to address what they believed to be the federal government's failure to secure the nation's borders. Although these measures received significant local support, they faced opposition from federal officials and civil rights groups. One of the first states to act was Arizona. In June 2007, Arizona lawmakers enacted a law that would suspend the business licenses of companies that knowingly hired illegal immigrants and mandated the use of the federal E-Verify program. The Justice Department challenged the law, arguing that federal law preempted state law. In May 2011, however, the Supreme Court upheld Arizona's law. Dissatisfied with the number of deportations, in 2010 Arizona also enacted State Bill 1070. This law authorized state and local police to determine the immigration status of those stopped, detained, or arrested, if officers reasonably suspected the person was unlawfully in the United States. The nationwide reaction on both sides of the immigration debate revealed just how contentious the issue had become. Supporters argued that states should have the right to secure their borders. The Justice Department opposed the law, claiming once again that federal law preempted state law. Civil rights organizations asserted that the law would promote racial profiling. Despite rather vocal opposition, the Supreme Court in June 2012 upheld what some call the "show me your papers" provision of the controversial law. Many fear the law will be challenging to enforce. According to *Colorlines* journalist Seth Freed Wessler, "There's no way for cops to know who's undocumented without profiling on the basis of race."[2] Despite these concerns, five other states—Utah, Indiana, Georgia, Alabama, and South Carolina—enacted similar laws.

The Barack Obama administration's strategy has combined strong enforcement with flexibility, which has met with some success. The CIS reported a record 396,906 illegal-immigrant removals during fiscal 2011. This number included court-ordered deportations and administrative or voluntary removals. Homeland Security also claims that the number of illegal crossings has dropped by more than half. Former de-

2. Seth Freed Wessler, "Supreme Court Upholds 'Show Me Your Papers' in Arizona's SB1070," *Colorlines*, June 25, 2012. http://colorlines.com/archives/2012/06/supreme_court_upholds_show_me_your_papers_in_sb_1070_blocks_other_provisions.html.

partment secretary Janet Napolitano linked the drop to the administration's policies. "The Obama administration has undertaken the most serious and sustained actions to secure our borders,"[3] Napolitano claimed. "It is clear from every measure we currently have that this approach is working,"[4] she added. Nevertheless, both those who support and oppose immigration question the administration's strategy. Mark Krikorian, executive director of the Center for Immigration Studies, an organization that opposes liberal immigration policies, does not deny the numbers; he questions the administration's commitment, as deportation numbers have begun to decline. However, those who support more open immigration policies believe the administration's enforcement policies are counterproductive. Janet Murguía, president of the National Council of La Raza, an immigrant advocacy organization, maintained, "As record levels of detention and deportation continue to soar, families are torn apart, innocent youth are being deported and children are left behind without the protection of their parents."[5]

In the eyes of many, efforts thus far to balance the benefits and challenges of immigration remain elusive. New hope seemed to emerge in January 2013, as eight senators, representing both parties, released a plan for immigration reform. On April 17, 2013, the Gang of Eight, as these senators came to be called, introduced Senate Bill 744—the Border Security, Economic Opportunity, and Immigration Modernization Act. Several key provisions reflect issues that continue to be of public concern on both sides of the border debate. The act requires strict monitoring of the border with the goal of turning

3. Janet Napolitano, "Homeland Security and Economic Security," January 30, 2012. www.dhs.gov/news/2012/01/30/secretary-homeland-security-janet-napolitanos-2nd -annual-address-state-americas.
4. *Ibid.*
5. Janet Murguía, "President and CEO of NCLR Responses to President Obama's Speech in El Paso Texas," May 10, 2011. www.nclr.org/index.php/about_us/news/ news_releases/janet_murgua_president_and_ceo_of_nclr_responds_to_president _obamas_speech_in_el_paso_texas.

back 90 percent of those who try to cross. On the other hand, it also creates a path to citizenship for those who meet specific criteria. The law requires business owners to use an electronic verification system to ensure legal hiring status. At the same time, the law overhauls how legal immigration is determined. However, not unlike the terrorist attacks that stalled immigration reform legislation early in the Bush administration, just days before the bill was introduced, three people were killed and hundreds injured in the Boston Marathon bombings.

In the days that followed the bombings, Americans learned that the alleged perpetrators were Chechen immigrants. The two suspects, brothers Tamerlan Tsarnaev and Dzhokar Tsarnaev, came to the United States along with their parents as refugees seeking asylum from persecution.[6] Although Chechens were subject to discrimination even before the fall of the Soviet Union, life became a nightmare for many after Russia invaded to end Chechnya's bid for independence when the Soviet Union dissolved. What concerned some American policy makers was information later released alleging that Tamerlan had become a follower of radical Islam. Despite warnings from Russian intelligence of Tamerlan's leanings, the FBI claimed to have investigated and found no evidence of terrorist activity. Nevertheless, these events lead some to fear that the recent immigration reform legislation will once again be deferred. Ross Baker, a congressional scholar at Rutgers University, said, "It would be very hard to argue to pass this thing immediately. The bombings give opponents a much more plausible reason to say, 'hold on, let's wait until all the facts are known,' which of course takes momentum out of the bill."[7]

---

6. Tamerlan was killed in a police shootout on April 19, 2013, and Dzhokar was wounded and fled but was later captured. On April 22, 2013, Dzhokar was charged with using and conspiring to use a weapon of mass destruction resulting in death and with malicious destruction of property resulting in death.

7. Quoted in Tracy Jan and Michael Kranish, "Fallout from Bombings Threatens Immigration Measure," *Boston Globe*, April 22, 2013.

The Boston bombings did indeed lead some opposed to open borders to challenge immigration reform. Senator Rand Paul, a Kentucky Republican and a leader of the Tea Party movement,[8] argued, "The facts emerging in the Boston Marathon bombing have exposed a weakness in our current system. If we don't use this debate as an opportunity to fix flaws in our current system, flaws made even more evident last week, then we will not be doing our jobs."[9] Also in his letter to the Senate majority leader Harry Reid, Paul maintained, "National security protections must be rolled into comprehensive immigration reform to make sure the federal government does everything it can to prevent immigrants with malicious intent from using our immigration system to gain entry into the United States in order to commit future acts of terror."[10]

Those who support more open borders argue that opponents misrepresent the facts surrounding the Chechen brothers to unnecessarily stall immigration reform. Libertarian policy analyst Shikha Dalmia argues that the two Chechen brothers obtained asylum in 2002 at the ages of eight and fifteen. At that time there was no evidence that Tamerlan would become a religious zealot. Indeed, she maintained, "Expecting the immigration system to predict that Tamerlan would become a lunatic is as reasonable as expecting psychiatrists to diagnose that Timothy McVeigh[11] would become a terrorist when he was a toddler. The lack of omniscience in human institutions is not a curable flaw."[12] While many agree that the need for background checks is essential, these analysts assert that restricting the flow of people is as dangerous as restricting the flow of ideas. As Dalmia states, "Shutting the border to economic migrants, whether computer geeks from China or

---

8. The Tea Party movement generally refers to those who believe in reducing US government spending, taxes, the national debt, and the federal budget deficit. This definition is limited, however, as the party has many factions and little structure. Some claim that the movement has divided the Republican party making it less effective.

9. Quoted in Jan and Kranish, *op. cit.*

10. Quoted in Jan and Kranish, *op. cit.*

apple-pickers from Mexico, in a vain effort to deter a future Tamerlan won't make Americans better off."[13] In fact, open border advocates contend, efforts to close US borders to particular groups of people are counterproductive. According to Kathleen Newland, director of the Migration Policy Institute's refugee protection program, "If US authorities had made a blanket decision that children from Russia were potential terrorists, they would have turned away 6-year-old Sergey Brin, the computer genius who co-founded Google, along with 8-year-old Dzhokar Tsarnaev."[14]

Until more is revealed about the Boston Marathon bombings, its impact on the most recent immigration reform strategy remains to be seen. From the 1980s to the present, however, whether the US borders should remain open or closed to the free flow of immigrants remains contentious, as are the viewpoints in *At Issue: Should the US Close Its Borders?* Some believe that the issue has become too politicized for reform, but others claim that changing national demographics make it impossible to ignore. Mary Giovagnoli, of the Immigration Policy Center, believes it will be a challenge. "I do believe we're going to reform the immigration system,"[15] she claimed. Nevertheless, Giovagnoli added, "Even under the best of circumstances, it's a lot of work."[16]

11. McVeigh was an American terrorist who on April 19, 1995, detonated a truck bomb in front of the Alfred P. Murrah Federal Building in Oklahoma City. The attack killed 168 people and injured over 800 and thus far is the deadliest act of domestic terrorism in US history.

12. Shikha Dalmia, "Anti-Immigration Conservatives Get Silly After Boston Bombings," *Reason*, April 30, 2013.

13. *Ibid.*

14. Kathleen Newland, "Reminder from Boston Marathon Bombings: A Need to Integrate Immigrant Children," *Christian Science Monitor*, April 29, 2013.

15. Quoted in Jost, *op. cit.*

16. Quoted in Jost, *op. cit.*

1

Continued Efforts to Close US Borders Are Necessary

Mark Krikorian

Mark Krikorian is executive director of the Center for Immigration Studies, a think tank that advocates immigration reduction.

Although illegal immigration has slowed, the US government must continue efforts to more effectively close the country's borders. In truth, poor economic conditions in the United States better explains the decline than enforcement measures. Thus, as the economic situation in the country improves so will the need for reforms, such as building better border barriers and adding staff to police them. In addition, the government should implement programs that require employers to verify the citizenship of new hires and add systems that better track foreign visitors. Moreover, to reduce the impact of immigration on American schools and public services and protect American jobs, agencies should actively enforce immigration laws.

There's broad agreement that the illegal-immigrant population peaked in 2007 and declined for the next two years. The three main sources of estimates—the Department of Homeland Security, the Pew Hispanic Center and the Center for Immigration Studies—all conclude that in 2007, the illegal population neared or exceeded twelve million (the estimates range from 11.8 to 12.5 million) and declined to roughly eleven million (between 10.8 and 11.1 million) by 2009. The decline stopped after 2009, so until new estimates or new facts are developed, it's safe to say that there are currently about eleven million unauthorized residents of the United States. Dramatically higher numbers sometimes bandied about by commentators and politicians—such as a 2005 estimate by Bear Stearns analysts that the illegal population could be as high as twenty million—are almost certainly incorrect. If the number were that high, it would be reflected in birth and death records, since in a modern society such as ours almost no one is born or dies without that fact being administratively recorded, and we have a pretty good idea of the fertility and mortality rates of the illegal population.

A Decline in Illegal Immigration

It seems clear that illegal crossings at the border, known formally as entries without inspection, are also down. Although illegal entry is not the only source of illegal immigrants—perhaps 40 percent of the illegal population entered legally on some kind of visa and then overstayed—it is the main source, and there's a lot less of it. The only administrative metric available for illegal crossings is the number of apprehensions made by the Border Patrol. This is an imperfect yardstick; a drop in apprehensions could mean there are fewer illegal immigrants available for agents to catch, or it could mean that the Border Patrol is becoming less efficient at finding them. Likewise, the total apprehensions number includes people who attempt to cross multiple times, though such recidivism appears to have declined slightly. It's possible, then, that a drop in apprehensions, coupled with a drop in recidivism, might not indicate a reduction in the actual number of individuals trying to sneak across the border.

But the decrease in the number of arrests at the border is sufficiently steep that the only plausible explanation is that attempted crossings have declined, and the experience of border residents confirms this. Arrests on the Mexican border exceeded one million almost every year since the early 1980s and totaled almost 1.2 million in 2005. In 2007, arrests were under nine hundred thousand. They dropped to a little over half a million in 2009 and 328,000 in 2011. That 2011 number is the lowest seen in the country since the early 1970s.

The Pew Hispanic Center has estimated that the total inflow of illegal immigrants, both border jumpers and visa overstayers, declined from 850,000 annually during 2000–2005 to just three hundred thousand annually during 2007–2009. The total number of illegal aliens declined despite a continued inflow of new illegal aliens because, over time, many people stop being illegal aliens. Some return home, some launder their status to become legal immigrants and a few die. Though researchers disagree, both statistical and anecdotal evidence suggests the number of illegal immigrants leaving the United States increased during the recession.

With regard to Mexico in particular, Pew has recently reported that net migration has dropped to zero. This includes all immigrants, both legal and illegal (51 percent of recent Mexican immigrants are illegal). Specifically, Pew compares the 2005–2010 period to 1995–2000 and finds that the number of Mexicans arriving in the United States fell by half and the number returning doubled. From 2005–2010, arrivals and departures were roughly equal, with each figure at about 1.4 million. The number of departures is fudged somewhat, since it includes three hundred thousand U.S.-born (and thus U.S. citizen) children of Mexican immigrants, so even Pew finds continued net Mexican immigration, but the increase in departures (most of them voluntary) and the drop in new arrivals is striking.

Explaining the Decline

There is little doubt that the annual flow of illegal immigrants has slowed and the total illegal population has shrunk somewhat, although eleven million illegal immigrants is still a very large number. While interesting, this fact on its own doesn't tell us much that can be applied to policy. It's necessary to explore the reasons for the decline. Three explanations have been offered: first, the recession; second, increased enforcement; and third, changes in Mexico, the source of roughly 60 percent of the illegal population. . . .

Of these three factors—the U.S. economy, an enhanced enforcement regime and Mexico's demographic shifts—the first is obviously the most changeable. The unemployment rate has already begun to decline, dropping from 9.1 percent in August 2011 to 8.2 percent in June of this year [2012]. GDP [gross domestic product] growth resumed in 2010 at an annual rate of 2.8 percent (though the 2011 rate was lower).

What's more, there's evidence that immigrants are capturing a disproportionate share of whatever new jobs are being created. A Center for Immigration Studies report looking specifically at Texas found that, from 2007 through the second quarter of 2011, 81 percent of job growth went to newly arrived immigrants, half of them illegal aliens.

Much needs to be done before the United States has the enforcement arrangements necessary to permanently reduce illegal immigration to a nuisance rather than an ongoing crisis.

Questioning the Impact of Border Enforcement

The vicissitudes of the economy obviously can't be relied on to limit illegal immigration. So to the degree that the economy is the cause for the current lull, it would seem to be temporary. That raises a question: Even with the return of strong job growth, would the new enforcement measures continue to blunt renewed pressure for illegal immigration?

President Obama's answer would appear to be yes. Speaking in El Paso last year [2011], he outlined various improvements in border enforcement, then mocked those still dissatisfied:

> But even though we've answered these concerns, I've got to say I suspect there are still going to be some who are trying to move the goal posts on us one more time. . . . You know, they said we needed to triple the Border Patrol. Or now they're going to say we need to quadruple the Border Patrol. Or they'll want a higher fence. Maybe they'll need a moat. Maybe they want alligators in the moat. They'll never be satisfied. And I understand that. That's politics.

Obama's mockery implies the country has done everything a nation can possibly do to control immigration, that the recent improvements complete the infrastructure necessary for border control and that it's time to move on to other things—namely, amnesty for the illegal immigrants already here and increases in future legal immigration.

Unfortunately, this is not true. Much needs to be done before the United States has the enforcement arrangements necessary to permanently reduce illegal immigration to a nuisance rather than an ongoing crisis. Start at the border. The increases in the Border Patrol over the past fifteen years have been real, but even at a staff level of twenty-one thousand, the agency—responsible for more than 7,500 miles of our land frontiers—is smaller than the New York City Police Department, which has 34,500 uniformed officers. Furthermore, the improvements in fencing are often exaggerated. Of the nearly seven hundred miles of physical barriers along our southern border, a large portion are Normandy barriers, designed to stop vehicular incursions across the border but of no use in stopping people on foot. What's more, when Congress passed the Secure Fence Act, it imagined double fencing of the kind south of San Diego. In fact, only about 1 percent of the border has a double layer.

This is why the Government Accountability Office reported last year that only 44 percent of the border is under "operational control," with only 15 percent actually "controlled" (the tightest level of security). That 44 percent figure is triple what it was in 2005, but it's hard to say a task is complete when it's not even half done.

> *Another potential valuable tool that is still not fully functional is a system to track all entries and exists by foreign visitors.*

Deceptive Deportation Record

The high level of deportations is likewise deceptive. The administration likes to boast of "record" deportations, but the other half of the story is that the growth in deportations has stopped. The reason annual deportations have been just under four hundred thousand during this administration is that the White House refuses to ask Congress for the funds to increase it further. Like the child on trial for killing his parents who then pleads for mercy as an orphan, the administration has created the very resource constraints it points to as the reason for not increasing deportations further.

Beyond that, some key enforcement tools remain unused. The E-Verify system[1] is working well, but its effectiveness is necessarily limited until it is required for all new hires. Regrettably, the president is holding that change hostage in exchange for amnesty for illegal immigrants. In other words, he (and many in both parties who share his perspective) will accept the tool needed to exclude illegal immigrants from the workforce only after amnesty has ensured there are no more illegal aliens left in the workforce.

---

1. The E-Verify system is an Internet-based system that allows businesses to determine the eligibility of their employees to work in the United States.

Another potentially valuable tool that is still not fully functional is a system to track all entries *and* exits by foreign visitors. As noted above, a large share of the illegal population was admitted legally in some sort of temporary status and never left. But despite a congressional mandate passed in the 1996 immigration-reform bill and reiterated by the 9/11 Commission, we still have no fully functional exit-tracking program and no plans to build one. The lack of such an elementary capability makes a mockery of the claim that our immigration infrastructure is complete.

Lack of sufficient enforcement [of illegal immigration] remains a problem.

A Lawless Approach

And then there's the problem of political will. Even the improvements we've put in place over the past fifteen years are of little benefit if they are not used properly. And the current administration has announced that, as a matter of policy, it will seek to arrest and deport only those illegal immigrants who have committed serious, nonimmigration offenses. In a series of memos encouraging agents in the field to exercise their "prosecutorial discretion," the administration made clear that it views illegal presence in the United States (and all its ancillary crimes, such as document fraud and identity theft) as a secondary offense, like not buckling your seat belt while driving. In other words, they seek to pursue immigration offenses only in conjunction with other crimes. That means they will deport a rapist after he has completed his U.S. prison sentence, but they are uninterested in ordinary illegal aliens.

While prioritizing limited resources is part of any enforcement regime, this wholesale downgrade of an entire body of law is unprecedented. It's as though the Internal Revenue Service were to announce that ordinary citizens who are not terrorists or money launderers don't need to comply with the tax law because, as a matter of policy, no one would pursue them. The unprecedented and even lawless nature of the administration's approach is perhaps why so many immigration agents in the field have simply refused to obey what they see as an illegal order—one even their labor union said they should resist.

A Lack of Sufficient Enforcement

Do these things matter if the supply of illegal immigrants is drying up? Unfortunately, lack of sufficient enforcement remains a problem. Lower fertility and declining population are no guarantee that emigration from Mexico will come to an end. Emigration is not analogous to an overflowing cup that stops spilling liquid when the level falls. Migration is based on networks of family, clan and village that can continue to operate long after the conditions that may have sparked the original emigration have disappeared. For example, the states of western-central Mexico—far from the border—that sent farmworkers in the 1940s and 1950s through the so-called bracero program are still disproportionately important sending areas nearly a lifetime after the program began.

> *The problems associated with illegal immigration . . . have nothing to do with legal status and everything to do with numbers.*

Looking at fertility rates in other countries confirms that low birthrates and low emigration are not necessarily connected. Mexico's current TFR [total fertility rate] is almost identical to that of other countries of emigration[2]—Burma

---

2. The author distinguishes between emigration, moving out of a country, and immigration, moving into another county, to highlight the differing conditions within a nation from which people emigrate from those conditions in the country to which they migrate.

and Indonesia—but also the same as countries of immigration—Saudi Arabia and Argentina. Likewise, South Korea and Russia have some of the lowest TFRs in the world—1.23 and 1.42, respectively. In fact, Russia's population is already declining and is expected to fall about 11 percent by midcentury. And yet both South Korea and Russia are major source countries for immigration to the United States. Though correlation doesn't necessarily imply causation, in both cases the U.S. immigrant populations from those countries have risen just as fertility rates have fallen.

And there's always the rest of the world. Mexicans account for more than half of the current illegal population, but close to another 20 percent comes from Central America, which is even poorer and less developed. And TFRs are still very high in much of Africa and the Middle East. The importance of networks means we get little immigration from, say, Chad, but the U.S. legal-immigration system, especially refugee resettlement and the visa lottery, actually creates new networks for future illegal immigration.

The Impact of Legal Immigration

As important as it is to have a functioning immigration-control program, legal immigration is ultimately more consequential. Of the forty million foreign-born people living in the United States, nearly three-quarters of them are legal. Even in 2008–2009, during the two years of the worst recession in living memory, 2.5 million people moved here from abroad, most of them legally. And the problems associated with illegal immigration—burdens on schools, pressure on public services, even wage suppression—have nothing to do with legal status and everything to do with numbers. For example, a fourth of all people in the United States living in poverty are immigrants (legal and illegal) and their young children. Immigrant families account for a third of the uninsured, while 36 percent of immigrant households use at least one federal welfare program.

Thus, there is no reason to conclude this big national crisis, or the intense political emotions it generates, will fade from the scene anytime soon. Those who think otherwise are engaging in wishful thinking, likely born of their own favorable view toward the immigration wave of recent decades. The problem is ongoing, as is the civic and political imperative that it be confronted.

2

Closing US Borders Is Immoral and Impractical

Seth Polley

Seth Polley is Border Missioner in the Episcopal Diocese of Arizona and Vicar of St. John's, Bisbee, and St. Stephen's, Douglas, Arizona.

The United States is a nation of immigrants and should welcome those who come here to escape poverty and improve their lives. The fact that the nation has traditionally welcomed immigrants explains at least in part its good fortune. Moreover, that people are willing to sacrifice so much to come to America serves as a reminder of the nation's abundance. Policies that keep family members apart and force those seeking a better way of life to risk death in America's deserts are immoral. Indeed, such policies create fear and division in border communities. Although the government should prevent those who would harm the United States from entering, these policies should discriminate between criminals and those who want to pursue the opportunities that make America a great nation.

Dick Armey, retired member of Congress, conservative Christian, and Tea Party activist, may have our answer. In a public conversation with Representative Tom Tancredo, who favors closing our doors to Mexican immigrants, Armey re-

Seth Polley, "Borders and Blessings: Reflections on the National Immigration Crisis from the Arizona Desert," *Anglican Theological Review*, vol. 92, no. 4, Fall 2010, pp. 731–738. Copyright © 2010 by Seth Polley. All rights reserved. Reproduced by permission.

minds us that this country has always held its doors open: "America's not a nation that builds walls." We don't build up walls in the United States. We tear them down.

Tearing Down Walls

Bishop Kirk Smith serves the Episcopal Diocese of Arizona, the state which includes the Tucson Sector, the heaviest drug and human trafficking south-to-north corridor in the United States. He regularly reminds his clergy and laity that the current immigration crisis we face is the civil rights struggle of this generation. For the past three years, he, along with Arizonan Episcopalians and others, has traveled to the sleepy Mexican pueblo of Naco, Sonora, for the annual "God Has No Borders" Naco Border Procession. Together with the bishop at the U.S.-Mexico border, we have listened as he has reminded all of us that "God hates walls," that "God tears down walls," that the wall between Mexico and the United States will one day be a part of the "ash heap of history" where remnants of other walls, Jericho's and Berlin's among them, gather dust and return to the soil.

Members of the Diocese of Arizona, along with other people of faith and local residents, recently held the 2010 Border Procession. This particular procession, the fifth annual, was exceptional. The event was a beautiful, binational celebration of people and culture. Those of us from the United States crossed into Mexico into a colorful array of music, welcome, and the green, white, and red of the Mexican flag. The entire community of Naco bid us welcome. We were called friends and neighbors and reminded that "God has no borders." We processed along the main street of Naco to sirens, praise music, and folkloric dance. The political persuasion of the U.S. participants in this event was diverse; their religious affiliation, in some cases, nonexistent. But unity was tangible and friendship real. The irony of the moment did not escape us. Many of the people of Naco knew that the state of Arizona had enacted only the day before a severe law created out of the fear of scarcity. Mexico's response, in contrast, extended to us a festive hospitality and a gracious and abundant welcome.

A Nation of Immigrants

Our nation, as everyone recognizes—even those opposed to immigration reform—is a nation of immigrants. Only the flora and fauna are indigenous to North America. Whether we arrived via the Bering Strait, Boston, or the U.S.-Mexico border, whether we came four hundred years ago or four days ago, we all began our journey elsewhere. We forget that at our peril. Throughout the history of the United States, several successive migration waves have contributed to our common life, helping to fashion us as a diverse, flexible, and tolerant society. Unquestionably, immigrants have experienced exploitation and abuses at the hands of those who preceded their arrival, and they in turn have acted out nativist impulses against others who followed them. But as a whole, immigrants have long been appreciated as contributing to the marvel of what this country has become: one from many. Acknowledging the debt we owe to our immigrant heritage is essential as we face the challenges the current immigration wave of Latino migrants present us.

The core values of our faith have always favored life and prosperity.

The vast majority of immigrants who look to the United States for a new home look north from the south, and the vast majority from Mexico. These immigrants flee not the destruction and ravages of war, but the slower decay and death of poverty. They look north for economic opportunity: most of them come here simply to have a better life, to work, to help family members still in the south, to give their children food and education and health care.

The immigration policy of our government does not welcome Latino migrants. The United States does not issue an adequate number of work visas, particularly for those who have few or no marketable skills. Those fortunate enough to acquire guest worker status often earn just enough to cover travel and living costs in the United States and can only save or send home modest remittances. Consequently, Latino immigrants come by the thousands and hundreds of thousands into the U.S. without benefit of legal status and documentation. They cross into the country illegally because they have little or no other choice. To stay in their own countries means continued poverty, lack of necessities, and decline. To venture to the north, toward opportunity, education, and economic well-being, despite the risks to their lives and the harsh separation from those they love, means life and hope.

We in the United States would do well to open our doors more widely.

Remembering Strangers

The core values of our faith have always favored life and prosperity. God promised Abraham he would father a great nation with descendants too numerous to count. Jesus shared with his followers and other hearers that he came to give them life abundant. Our tradition has always asked us to remember the poor and share the good life with others from our own abundance. It also insists that we remember those who, because of widowhood or status as orphans or identity as strangers, do not have the ability to share in the abundance around them. Through its Levitical code, Israel asked itself to remember the strangers among them. Once they possessed Canaan, they were not to forget the burdens they bore as they made Pharaoh's bricks, not to forget what it was to be a stranger in a strange land. To do so was to risk forgetting who they were as God's people.

So much emphasis in our church conversations has centered on sexuality and debates around appropriate sexual conduct. Many reference two single Levitical injunctions against what is perceived as aberrant sexual behavior (Lev. 18:22, 20:13). Little attention, in comparison, is given to the same Levitical code which urges Israel to remember the stranger, to care for the alien, and to welcome the sojourner (Lev. 19:10, 33–34; 23:22). Such a contrast in emphasis prompts the question, "Why was it so important to Israel to establish this ethic and to insist upon supporting the stranger?"

Israel reminded itself to welcome and care for the stranger precisely because it did not experience such embrace and generosity in Egypt. Israel was to remember by welcoming; to remember by never forgetting its past and God's powerful work in delivering its people out of that suffering. Doing so strengthened God's chosen and encouraged them to be the people of God they knew themselves to be and to build the society worthy of that identity.

Opening Doors

We in the United States would do well to open our doors more widely. The faith that many possess here and the morality that anchors it require us to prevent deaths in the desert, to reunite families, and to offer people a living wage. The parable of the sheep and the goats in Matthew 25 is only one example of passages in Scripture that support our efforts to care for the stranger among us. Our values require nothing less from us.

National self-interest, however, also compels us to open our doors. Though not at the heart of our faith system nor particularly emphasized by the One we follow as Lord, self-interest needs to be appreciated and well-articulated if we are to speak with any relevance to other citizens of our country who play a crucial role in bringing about immigration reform.

Many people on this planet covet and envy our abundance and look at our democratic and economic success as something to be emulated. The United States boasts one of the largest middle classes in history and enjoys a political system that is relatively responsive to the wishes of those it governs— the recent immigration law in Arizona being an unfortunate and sad proof of such political agility. Many of us here earn a decent living, have quality health care and enough food to eat, and are able to educate our children well. Other people see our wealth and go to great extremes to share in our prosperity.

Including Others

The practice of including others into our society, economy, and civic institutions explains, in part, our good fortune. Even though longstanding racial tensions and economic disparities befuddle and weaken us, the United States continues to be a tolerant society. Our abundance includes a free press, a relatively transparent system of government, civilian control of our military, and an economic system capable of great flexibility and the creation of immense wealth.

> *With reasonable immigration policy in place, migrants could work in the legitimate economy and participate in the assimilation process.*

An embrace of immigrants, of those looking to do better for themselves and their families, helps to explain this public good. Whether they were Puritans escaping religious intolerance, Irish fleeing famine, or Jews and others rejecting Nazism, people have come here seeking to leave tyranny, however manifest, behind. In abandoning the limitations of their home country, immigrants have found opportunity leading to the creation of wealth. Europeans from southern and eastern Europe, for example, contributed their labor to the country's industrialization in the eighteenth and nineteenth centuries. And as they worked, they participated in and created our civic institutions, faith communities, and governments. Many problems abound for us today, such as how to continue to cultivate the kind of cultural miscegenation [mixture of races] that contributes to a creative and open society, but our nation's strength derives from its immigrant foundation.

We are stronger as a people each time a new resident succeeds in education, business, and family life. When we succumb to the fear of scarcity, relationships are perceived as a burden rather than a gift. New opportunities can be obscured or missed because of the perception that there is or will not be enough. Growth and welcome and inclusion are hard work and lead to unforeseen and heavy challenges. The integration of culture and language often unearths differing historical perspectives and our understandings and theologies, once dominant and privileged, sometimes resist leveling and competition. To resist this essential grafting process, however, can produce even greater difficulty and danger: stagnation, closed-mindedness, and insularity.

A Need for Broad Reform

Opponents of immigration reform point out that to "open our borders" will release an inundation of unskilled migrants who will overburden our educational and health care infrastructure to the point of collapse. But the reality here in Arizona and elsewhere is that we already are experiencing an inundation of migrants. Our border is porous. Those who are not apprehended still manage to cross into the United States, but they do not have the benefit of adequate legal protections from unfair practices in the workplace, and they are forced to live on the fringes of society. With reasonable immigration policy in place, migrants could work in the legitimate economy and participate in the assimilation process, which has contributed immeasurable good to our country and could work in our favor once again. Additionally, with reform in place, law enforcement personnel, who are currently heavily burdened by the apprehension, processing, and deportation of economic migrants, could be redirected and their time reallocated toward illegal drug interdiction and the capture and prosecution of real and dangerous criminals. Efforts could also be redoubled to assure that those who threaten terror are unsuccessful at crossing into our country at its southern border.

> *Immigrants from all countries, but especially those from across our southern border, remind us of what we underappreciate and undervalue.*

Without broad reform our situation will worsen, and more states, out of a growing sense of frustration, panic, and anxiety, will pass laws that exacerbate the crisis rather than solve it, as we have seen in Arizona. Senate Bill 1070 mandates that Arizona local police and sheriff departments must enforce federal immigration law, which will only worsen an already tenuous relationship between residents and the police. Undocumented residents, and their friends and families, will no longer report crimes against them, fearing that to do so will subject them to scrutiny of their own immigration status. Effective law enforcement depends on a basic trust between the residents of a community and the officers who protect it. If even a small segment of a community does not report robbery, rape, and other serious crimes, all the inhabitants of that community live in greater danger. Bombs and violence, though powerful and real, are no match for subtler vehicles of death and destruction: silence, intolerance, and fear of the other.

Remembering Our History

In his final Deuteronomic discourse, Moses called the Israelites to choose life and blessing, abundance and relationship, as they entered into the promised land (Deuteronomy 30). He urged Israel to move into its future confident in their covenant with God and conscious of their experience as a people called, delivered, saved. Moses reminded his people that their survival depended on their appreciation of what God had done in their history. They could not create their future as a free and prosperous nation without remembering their past as suffering slaves, and God's powerful, concrete, and defining intervention. That memory would serve them as they faced abundance and lack, war and exile, restoration and hope.

As we make way for the stranger among us, as we enact humane and just immigration reform, we are doing this as much unto ourselves as unto others. Immigrants from all countries, but especially those from across our southern border, remind us of what we underappreciate and undervalue. They remind us that there is still milk and honey here in this land of promise. They remind us that if people are supported and allowed to pursue opportunity, to use their imagination, to learn and to work well, good things can and will happen.

Stories of Success

Many anecdotes circulate among those of us who live on the U.S.-Mexico border. One such story tells of an immigrant who turned abandoned wooden pallets into a profitable business simply by retrieving them from trash dumps, repairing them, and selling them to new users. An Episcopalian in Arizona tells his story as the son of a woman who left her family in Mexico and crossed into the United States hoping to find work enough to send for her children. When she found that work, she sent for her children, and they all benefited from the 1986 federal legislation that legalized their immigration status. Her children received an excellent education, and they are currently raising their own families. They share their faith with their children, encourage them to care about their neighborhoods, teach them to vote, to pay taxes, to enjoy abundance, and remind them to care for others less fortunate than themselves. As with earlier waves of migration, this current wave has and will continue to contribute good to our society in measurable and concrete ways.

At our best, we do well to make room for others, to welcome, to help people to find a place. The myth of Israel, the myth of the United States, our own personal family and individual myths—they remind us of what is possible here, and what can be done with creativity and imagination and the support of the law. They remind us of one of the fundamental truths of who we are as a people: that there is promise among us, or, to use a theological term, blessing.

This current wave of migration will, if embraced, lead to a deeper and renewed sense of who we are as a people and a deeper commitment to our values.

The Danger of Forgetting

Blessing is what this current wave of Latino migration affords us: the blessing of those who look to this land and see what we are in danger of forgetting—that we in the United States have abundance and great blessing. We witness to the truth that what is held in common by a diverse society is stronger than what threatens to separate it. Social scientists and politicians point to the aging of the Anglo population in the United States, while acknowledging the relative youth of the Latino population. Our economic recovery and long-term interests are well-served by doing the very best we can to train and equip these younger people to lead and create in our economy.

I have seen what I argue for in the larger, national scope of our common life come to fruition on the local level in the bilingual congregation I serve on the border. At our bishop's request, St. Stephen's Church in Douglas, Arizona, instituted a Spanish service in 2007. Prior to this date our congregation was primarily Anglo and aging; other than Sunday mornings, it gathered infrequently for community events. With the addition of Spanish worship, as we seek to be one community that worships in two languages, a growing richness is surfacing as members from both services get to know each other and work and minister side by side. Challenges abound, such as the occasional and cumbersome bilingual worship service. Stewardship and giving needs to be strengthened. We do not educate our children as well as we could. But there is a real hope that the addition of our Spanish-speaking members will contribute to the long-term viability of this community of faith.

The Gift of Difference

This current wave of migration will, if embraced, lead to a deeper and renewed sense of who we are as a people and a deeper commitment to our values. At St. Stephen's, differences in languages and culture, typically seen as barriers, are increasingly appreciated as gift and blessing. These newcomers to the Episcopal Church have helped to give me, a lifelong Episcopalian, a renewed confidence and appreciation for the unique identity we possess as Anglicans. A similar dynamic can be true in the church at the national level, and regarding our civic life. Working with politically engaged immigrants renews my confidence in the democratic process. Their growing civic literacy challenges and encourages my own level of participation in public affairs. Enthusiasm is contagious, and our public life and institutions will grow stronger from those discovering their possibilities.

At St. Stephen's in Douglas, Arizona, a small church in a small town, we have new life because we have opened our doors, hung out our shingle, and welcomed those who once were strangers. Our challenges and resistances exist, but they are no match for blessing and life. God has asked us to remember: to remember that we all were far off once, but now have been brought near; to remember that the dividing walls of hostility between us, whether from the attitudes created by racial difference or culture or the fear that there will not be enough, will not last. Christ is our peace; we have crossed over into a new land of relationship, wonder, and opportunity where there are no walls. God has no borders. You and I are one.

3

Keeping US Borders Open Increases Crime and Terrorism

Jim Kouri

Jim Kouri, vice president of the National Association of Chiefs of Police, has served as director of security for a number of organizations and trained police and security officers throughout the country. He writes for police and crime magazines and appears as an on-air commentator.

Evidence reveals that Islamic terrorists are active in Central and South America, as well as Canada, and hope to enter the United States. Indeed, open US borders make Americans vulnerable to terrorists and other criminals. Drug cartels and the Mexican federal agents that pursue them sometimes enter the United States, putting border patrol agents who have no guidelines in place to respond to these incursions at risk. Weak border security also plays a part in domestic crime. In fact, a majority of the felony warrants in Los Angeles are for illegal aliens. Thus, to prevent terrorists and criminals from entering and putting Americans at risk, the United States should better defend its borders.

As the number of Americans who remember the horror of the terrorist attacks in New York and Washington almost eight years ago [2001] dwindles, the US borders are practically as porous as ever—and the terrorists know it. Even while President Barack Obama is in the Middle East wooing Islamic nations, Islamofascism is taking hold in Central and South America.

According to testimony given to the US House of Representatives Armed Services Committee by General Peter Pace, the former US Joint Chiefs of Staff, Hamas has joined Hezbollah and Al-Qaeda in the Triple Frontier Zone in Latin America where the borders of Argentina, Brazil and Paraguay converge.

There the Islamic terror groups train recruits, gather intelligence on targets, launder money and sell drugs. There is evidence that these terrorists and narco-terrorists will soon migrate north into the United States. He cited terrorism reports indicating terrorist groups are active in Canada and Central-South America.

Attacks on US Sovereignty

Border Patrol agents began to voice what many believed were legitimate concerns about "armed incursions" into the United States from Mexico-based assailants. They reported that heavily armed Mexican army units and federal police, called federales, had infiltrated US territory and fired upon them, in some cases. Mexican drug lords had put prices on the heads of American law-enforcement agents strung out along the border. Where was the outrage by our political leaders and the mainstream media over this blatant violation of our national sovereignty?

Last year [2008] I reported on armed Mexicans entering the US causing National Guard troops to retreat because they had limited, if any, rules of engagement. The federal government attempted to suppress the information of this incursion and violation of US sovereignty.

In Los Angeles, a look at outstanding arrest warrants for homicide reveals that over 90% are for illegal aliens.

Many of our political leaders and most in the news media ignore these violent attacks on our national sovereignty while more and more Americans are saying, "This has got to stop!"

Some security experts had high hopes that President Bush would bring up the border security problem during his meeting with then Mexican President Vincente Fox. It never happened. Quite the opposite occurred. The two leaders discussed ways of relaxing immigration restrictions including a de facto amnesty program. Now with President Barack Obama and the Democrat Party in charge of two branches of government, observers believe even less will be done to secure our borders.

Putting aside terrorism, the lack of border security contributes to crime. In Los Angeles, a look at outstanding arrest warrants for homicide reveals that over 90% are for illegal aliens. Examination of all LA felony arrest warrants (murder, rape, armed robbery, etc.) shows that 65% are for illegal aliens. The Manhattan Institute estimates that 350 killers managed to escape back into Mexico and the Mexican government refuses to extradite to the US to stand trial. In another study, a sample group of 55,000 criminal aliens committed 700,000 criminal acts.

And our northern border with Canada has many law-enforcement leaders even more concerned. Canadian security experts concede that there are several radical Islamist groups active in their country. In fact, Hezbullah's largest headquarters is located not in the Middle East but in Toronto. One Canadian intelligence officer claims that his country's immigration policy is more lax than US policy and their politicos more liberal when it comes to refusing to restrict illegal aliens from entering Canada.

If these killers aren't afraid to target or kill cops, then who in America is really safe from terrorists, murderers, rapists and other offenders; and anyone wishing to address the problem is labeled a racist or xenophobe. Americans can probably count on one hand the number of congressional leaders who will even debate the issues of illegal immigration or border security.

What sense does it make to inspect shipping containers in New York seaports while ignoring the vulnerabilities existing on our borders?

Nuclear Smuggling

In a previous column, I reported on how easily it was for undercover investigators to sneak radioactive material—to be used for "dirty bombs"—into the US.

The undercovers were successful at both borders 100% of the time. Yet, the White House, Congress and the news media ignored the subsequent report from the Government Accountability Office about the undercover operation that proved we could not prevent weapons of mass destruction from being smuggled into the US.

Meanwhile, President Barack Obama is on his Middle East apology tour.

4

Keeping US Borders Open Will Not Increase Crime

Radley Balko

Radley Balko, a contributing editor at Reason *magazine, was policy analyst specializing in civil liberties issues for the libertarian Cato Institute. He also maintains a personal blog, TheAgitator.com.*

Contrary to oft-repeated claims connecting immigration and crime, studies reveal that cities with large immigrant populations are some of the safest cities in the United States. Immigrants are in fact less likely to commit crimes than native citizens. Indeed, most immigrants come to the United States at great cost and are therefore highly invested in their communities. Moreover, the opportunities available in the United States motivate immigrants to succeed. In truth, how host communities receive immigrants seems to better forecast crime. Thus, policy makers should take note that cities such as El Paso, Texas, one of the safest cities in the country, embrace their immigrant population.

By conventional wisdom, El Paso, Texas, should be one of the scariest cities in America. In 2007, the city's poverty rate was a shade over 27 percent, more than twice the national average. Median household income was $35,600, well below the national average of $48,000. El Paso is three-quarters Hispanic, and more than a quarter of its residents are foreign-born. Given that it's nearly impossible for low-skilled immigrants to work in the United States legitimately, it's safe to say that a significant percentage of El Paso's foreign-born population is living here illegally.

El Paso also has some of the laxer gun control policies of any non-Texan big city in the country, mostly due to gun-friendly state law. And famously, El Paso sits just over the Rio Grande from one of the most violent cities in the western hemisphere, Ciudad Juarez, Mexico, home to a staggering 2,500 homicides in the last 18 months alone. A city of illegal immigrants with easy access to guns, just across the river from a metropolis ripped apart by brutal drug war violence. Should be a bloodbath, right?

Surprisingly Crime-Free Border Cities

Here's the surprise: There were just 18 murders in El Paso last year, in a city of 736,000 people. To compare, Baltimore, with 637,000 residents, had 234 killings. In fact, since the beginning of 2008, there were nearly as many El Pasoans murdered while visiting Juarez (20) than there were murdered in their home town (23).

> *San Diego, Laredo, El Paso—these cities are teeming with immigrants, and they're some of the safest places in the country.*

El Paso is among the safest big cities in America. For the better part of the last decade, only Honolulu has had a lower violent crime rate (El Paso slipped to third last year, behind New York). *Men's Health* magazine recently ranked El Paso the second "happiest" city in America, right after Laredo, Texas—another border town, where the Hispanic population is approaching 95 percent.

So how has this city of poor immigrants become such an anomaly? Actually, it may not be an anomaly at all. Many criminologists say El Paso isn't safe despite its high proportion of immigrants, it's safe *because* of them.

Safe Cities Teeming with Immigrants

"If you want to find a safe city, first determine the size of the immigrant population," says Jack Levin, a criminologist at Northeastern University in Massachusetts. "If the immigrant community represents a large proportion of the population, you're likely in one of the country's safer cities. San Diego, Laredo, El Paso—these cities are teeming with immigrants, and they're some of the safest places in the country."

An immigrant group's propensity for criminality may be partly determined by how they're received in their new country.

If you regularly listen to talk radio, or get your crime news from anti-immigration pundits, all of this may come as a surprise. But it's not to many of those who study crime for a living. As the national immigration debate heated up in 2007, dozens of academics who specialize in the issue sent a letter to then President George W. Bush and congressional leaders with the following point:

> Numerous studies by independent researchers and government commissions over the past 100 years repeatedly and consistently have found that, in fact, immigrants are less likely to commit crimes or to be behind bars than are the native-born. This is true for the nation as a whole, as well as for cities with large immigrant populations such as Los Angeles, New York, Chicago, and Miami, and cities along the U.S.-Mexico border such as San Diego and El Paso.

One of the signatories was Rubén G. Rumbaut, a sociologist who studies immigration at the University of California, Irvine. Rumbaut recently presented a paper on immigration and crime to a Washington, D.C. conference sponsored by the Police Foundation. Rumbaut writes via email, "The evidence points overwhelmingly to the same conclusion: Rates of crime and conviction for undocumented immigrants are far below those for the native born, and that is especially the case for violent crimes, including murder."

Perpetuating Illegal Immigrant Myths

Opponents of illegal immigration usually do little more than cite andecdotes attempting to link illegal immigration to violent crime. When they do try to use statistics, they come up short. Rep. Steve King (R-Iowa), for example, has perpetuated the popular myth that illegal immigrants murder 12 Americans per day, and kill another 13 by driving drunk. King says his figures come from a Government Accountability Office [GAO] study he requested, which found that about 27 percent of inmates in the federal prison system are non-citizens. Colorado Media Matters looked into King's claim, and found his methodology lacking. King appears to have conjured his talking point by simply multiplying the annual number of murders and DWI [Driving While Intoxicated] fatalities in America by 27 percent. Of course, the GAO report only looked at federal prisons, not the state prisons and local jails where most convicted murderers and DWI offenders are kept. The Bureau of Justice Statistics puts the number of non-citizens (including legal immigrants) in state, local, and federal prisons and jails at about 6.4 percent. Of course, even that doesn't mean that non-citizens account for 6.4 percent of murders and DWI fatalities, only 6.4 percent of the overall inmate population.

What's happening with Latinos is true of most immigrant groups throughout U.S. history. "Overall, immigrants have a stake in this country, and they recognize it," Northeastern University's Levin says. "They're really an exceptional sort of American. They come here having left their family and friends back home. They come at some cost to themselves in terms of security and social relationships. They are extremely success-oriented, and adjust very well to the competitive circumstances in the United States." Economists Kristin Butcher and Anne Morrison Piehl argue that the very process of migration tends to select for people with a low potential for criminality.

How Immigrants Are Received

Despite the high profile of polemicists such as Lou Dobbs and Michael Savage, America has been mostly welcoming to this latest immigration wave. You don't see "Latinos Need Not Apply" or "No Mexicans" signs posted on public buildings the way you did with the Italians and the Irish, two groups who actually *were* disproportionately likely to turn to crime. The implication makes sense: An immigrant group's propensity for criminality may be partly determined by how they're received in their new country.

"Look at Arab-Americans in the Midwest, especially in the Detroit area," Levin says. "The U.S. and Canada have traditionally been very willing to welcome and integrate them. They're a success story, with high average incomes and very little crime. That's not the case in Europe. Countries like France and Germany are openly hostile to Arabs. They marginalize them. And they've seen waves of crime and rioting."

El Paso may be a concentrated affirmation of that theory. In 2007 the *Washington Post* reported on city leaders' wariness of anti-immigration policies coming out of Washington. The city went to court (and lost) in an effort to prevent construction of the border fence within its boundaries, and local officials have resisted federal efforts to enlist local police for immigration enforcement, arguing that it would make illegals less likely to cooperate with police. "Most people in Washington really don't understand life on the border," El Paso Mayor John Cook told the *Post*. "They don't understand our philosophy here that the border joins us together, it doesn't separate us."

Other mayors could learn something from Cook. El Paso's embrace of its immigrants might be a big reason why the low-income border town has remained one of the safest places in the country.

5

Open Borders Improve the US Economy

Gordon H. Hanson

Gordon H. Hanson is a professor of economics at the University of California San Diego and the director of the Center on Emerging and Pacific Economies who writes often on immigration issues.

Open border policies that encourage immigration promote economic growth. High-skilled immigrants produce innovative new products that increase the country's productivity. Immigration policies should therefore encourage talented students to stay in the United States to continue making economic contributions. Low-skilled immigrants also contribute to productivity by performing domestic jobs that free up American workers to occupy high-skilled positions. The mobility of low-skilled immigrant workers also smoothes economic fluctuations in struggling communities. In truth, efforts to reduce illegal immigration are costly. Since the impact on public services remains unclear, making it easier for immigrants to participate in the American economy will lead to more economic benefits than costs.

Ignoring immigration may make short-run political sense but it is a mistake if the goal is to build a coherent economic strategy. Immigration policy affects the pace of innovation in the U.S. economy, the supply of labor by high-skilled workers, the ability of regional economies to adjust to busi-

Gordon H. Hanson, "Immigration and Economic Growth," *Cato Journal*, vol. 32, no. 1, Winter 2012, pp. 25–34. Copyright © 2012 by The Cato Institute. All rights reserved. Reproduced by permission.

ness cycle fluctuations, and the integrity of local, state, and federal government finances. While current policies tend to do a poor job on these counts, designing a system that would make immigration good for America is easily within reach.

The Role of Immigration in Innovation

Past improvements in living standards for American households have been largely the consequence of growth in the productivity of capital and labor. Productivity growth, in turn, is the result of innovations that create new products and production processes. The Windows operating system, the iPhone, Lipitor and other cholesterol-reducing drugs, safe, fuel-efficient automobiles, and improved agricultural varieties are a few among the many new products that have appeared in recent decades and that have raised the level of national welfare. Each was the consequence of intensive research and development that culminated in a blockbuster product based on myriad new patents. A binding constraint in generating innovations is the supply of highly talented scientists, engineers, and other technical personnel. Immigration helps relax this constraint.

Each year, U.S. universities conduct a global talent search for the brightest minds to admit to their graduate programs. Increasingly, foreign students occupy the top spots in the search. Data from the National Science Foundation's Survey of Earned Doctorates show that between 1960 and the late 2000s, the share of PhDs awarded to foreign students rose from one fifth to three fourths in mathematics, computer science, and engineering; from one fifth to three fifths in physical sciences; and from one fifth to one half in life sciences. U.S. university departments that have more foreign graduate students produce more academic publications and have their work cited more frequently. Once they graduate, U.S.-educated foreign workers patent at a significantly higher rate than U.S.-born workers. As a consequence, U.S. cities that attract these workers produce larger numbers of patents in electronics, machinery, pharmaceuticals, industrial chemicals, and other technology-intensive products. Simply put, high-skilled immigration promotes innovation. An additional benefit is that high-skilled immigrants are likely to pay far more in taxes than they use in public services, generating a positive net contribution to government fiscal accounts.

Despite many hurdles to their entry, high-skilled immigrants make important contributions to U.S. productivity growth.

Attracting and Keeping Talented Foreigners

What does the United States do to attract talented foreigners? Foreign students who are admitted to U.S. universities can generally obtain a student visa. While the process of awarding visas was beset by onerous new restrictions after 9/11, many of these problems have since been resolved. Today, the difficulty is not in attracting top foreign students to America but in keeping here them after they graduate.

High-skilled immigrants have three primary channels for obtaining permission to work in the United States. The H-1B visa, which targets highly trained professionals, permits holders to work in the United States for a period of three years. It is renewable once, with the annual number of visas capped at 65,000. Employer-sponsored green cards permit holders to live and work in the country indefinitely. The annual number of new visas is capped at 150,000. The third channel is a family-sponsored green card, which requires marrying a U.S. citizen (visas for which there is no cap) or having a close relative already in the country legally (visas for which are capped at 640,000). Because of the limited number of work-based visas, the family visa route remains the most common path to legal residence for skilled workers. [Mark] Rosenzweig (2007) reports that in the early 2000s among immigrants who entered the United States on student visas and ultimately obtained green cards, 55 percent did so by marrying a U.S. citizen. To make it in America, foreign students not only need to be smart enough to get into a U.S. university. They also need to be proficient at dating.

Despite many hurdles to their entry, high-skilled immigrants make important contributions to U.S. productivity growth. By making it easier for talented foreign students to stay on in the country once their studies are finished, their contributions could be even larger.

Greasing the Wheels of the US Labor Market

Opposition to immigration in the United States is strongest regarding the admission of foreigners with low skill levels. There is the perception that low-skilled immigrants tend to be in the country illegally, to pay little in taxes while absorbing much in the way of government services, and to make neighborhoods less safe. Less appreciated are the contributions that low-skilled immigrants make in improving the efficiency of the U.S. economy. To use the words of George Borjas (2001), low-skilled immigration greases the wheels of the U.S. labor market.

One contribution of low-skilled immigrants is to make it possible for high-skilled workers to spend more time on the job and less time doing non-work related chores. Women account for an ever increasing share of the U.S. high-skilled labor force. In 2008, 48 percent of workers with a college degree were female (as were 54 percent of currently enrolled undergraduate students, meaning the female share of highly educated labor is likely to rise in the future). The majority of highly educated women are married to highly educated men. For both to work outside the home often requires hiring outside labor to care for children, clean the home, launder clothes, and tend to the yard. In a study of immigration's impact on U.S. cities, [Patricia] Cortes (2008) finds that metropolitan areas that have had larger influxes of low-skilled immigrants have lower prices for dry cleaning, child care, housing cleaning, yard care, and other labor-intensive services. Lower prices for these services translate into more hours spent at work for high-skilled workers, particularly among women with a professional degree or PhD. Low-skilled immigration thus indirectly contributes to productivity growth by raising the effective supply of high-skilled labor.

Increasing the Mobility of Labor

Another consequence of low-skilled immigration is to increase the mobility of the labor force. Low-skilled U.S.-born workers tend to be immobile across regions. When, say, the demand for low-skilled labor picks up in North Carolina, native-born workers in other regions are slow to move in. Why this is the case is poorly understood. The consequence of the immobility of low-skilled labor is to gum up the labor market, slowing the pace of growth in booming regions and the pace of recovery in slumping regions. Relative to low-skilled natives, low-skilled immigrants are more mobile geographically. They may hang dry wall in Texas in the winter, clean and pack poultry in Arkansas in the spring, and harvest vegetables in Georgia in the summer. True, many of these workers are in the country illegally. Approximately three-fifths of immigrant workers with less than a high school education are undocumented. Yet, their mobility across jobs and zip codes helps smooth fluctuations in the U.S. economy and ease the burden on U.S. workers when the unemployment rate rises. Since the last U.S. business cycle peak in 2007, the population of illegal immigrants has declined by about one million individuals. Many of those workers returned to their home countries after jobs in U.S. industries disappeared during the Great Recession. Flexibility in the employment of immigrant labor helps reduce volatility in employment for native labor. Undocumented workers are particularly flexible as they lack restrictions on moving between employers to which low-skilled workers on H-2A or H-2B temporary visas are subject.

Not all workers in the United States benefit from low-skilled immigration. While employers see their factories and farms become more productive and high-skilled workers enjoy lower prices for goods and services they purchase, low-skilled native-born workers face increased competition in the workplace. [George J.] Borjas (2003) finds that during the 1980s and 1990s low-skilled immigration reduced the wages of U.S.-born high-school dropouts by nine percent. Not all economists agree with his findings and the wage impact of immigration remains a topic of academic debate. Still, it is hard to imagine how more low-skilled immigration could be good for low-skilled native workers in the United States.

When assessing the labor market consequences of low-skilled immigration, it is important to keep in mind that any wage losses to low-skilled native workers represent a change in the *distribution* of national income but not in the *level* of national income. If low-skilled immigration pushes down wages for low-skilled labor, U.S. employers gain and U.S. low-skilled workers lose, with the gains to the former offsetting the losses to the latter. Moreover, economic theory suggests that immigration generates a surplus by making capital and land more productive, meaning that gains to U.S. employers are likely to exceed any losses to U.S. workers. In practice, the immigration surplus from low-skilled immigration in the United States appears to be small. But the point remains that one shouldn't count wage losses to low-skilled immigrant workers as a net loss from immigration, however painful it might be for the individuals who are negatively affected.

Immigration and the Tax Burden

Immigration's impact on government spending attracts much attention but is not well understood. A common criticism of immigration is that it increases government spending. If true, reducing immigration, and illegal immigration in particular, would help to narrow the scope of government. The relationship between immigration and public finances is complex. Under current tax and spending rules, an exodus of low-skilled immigrants probably would reduce the net burden on U.S. taxpayers. But if reducing immigration requires substantially higher levels of enforcement the drain on government budgets could actually increase. A more sensible approach than a pure-enforcement strategy would be to allow low-skilled immigration to occur but to shield taxpayers from negative effects.

If the extra cost of [additional immigration] enforcement is larger than the net fiscal cost of illegal immigration, then driving illegal immigration to zero would fail a cost-benefit test.

Low-skilled immigrants, whether legal or illegal, pay taxes and use government services. They pay sales taxes when they make purchases and property taxes for the housing they rent or own. A worker who presents a Social Security number to an employer, be the number valid or not, will have payroll taxes deducted from his or her paycheck, with those taxes sent on to the federal government. All workers are subject to federal income taxes, though in practice most low-income workers owe little in tax and most illegal workers appear not to file tax returns. To be eligible to receive welfare benefits financed by the federal government, an individual must be a U.S. citizen. Not only are illegal immigrants excluded from receiving federally funded entitlements but so are noncitizen legal immigrants. The major drain on government finances from immigration comes from public education—all children, regardless of legal status, must attend school—and public health care. The U.S.-born children of immigrants are eligible to receive Medicaid and other subsidized health services. Some ineligible immigrants obtain health services through hospital emergency rooms, often at public expense.

The net fiscal impact of low-skilled immigration is the subject of heated debate. Poring over the many recent studies—most of which offer only partial views of immigration's fiscal consequences and produce estimates that require strong assumptions that are difficult to verify—it does appear that the net fiscal impact is negative (CBO 2007). In the mid-2000s, [Steven A.] Camarota (2004) put the annual fiscal cost for the federal government at $12 billion (in 2011 dollars), with the net fiscal cost for state and local governments (whose total budgets are far less than the federal budget) exceeding this amount. Yet, even if these figures are true, it does not necessarily follow that the correct policy response is to attempt to eliminate illegal immigration.

The Cost of Policing US Borders

One problem with reducing low-skilled immigration is that doing so is not costless. Lowering the illegal population requires devoting more resources to policing U.S. borders and monitoring U.S. worksites. Even though in the last seven years the U.S. Border Patrol has more than doubled the number of officers on the U.S.-Mexico border (to 20,000 agents), illegal immigration continues. Encouraging the departure of the 11 million illegal immigrants currently in the country would require substantially more intensive interior enforcement. Immigration and Customs Enforcement has increased scrutiny of U.S. businesses and more and more employers use E-Verify to validate the eligibility of prospective workers for employment. But we still have around eight million undocumented workers in the U.S. labor force. Driving illegal immigration to zero would require additional enforcement at additional expense. If the extra cost of such enforcement is larger than the net fiscal cost of illegal immigration, then driving illegal immigration to zero would fail a cost-benefit test. In truth, we don't know if current levels of enforcement spending are justified. The 2011 combined budgets of Customs and Border Protection and Immigration and Customs Enforcement, the two federal agencies charged with immigration enforcement, was $15 billion, with not all of these funds going to immigration-related activities. Before ramping up enforcement further, the U.S. government should tell the American people exactly how much immigration enforcement costs and how much it saves taxpayers by removing immigrants who would otherwise be a net fiscal burden on the U.S. economy. To date, the government has failed to provide such information.

For the United States immigration of high-skilled labor accelerates the rate of productivity growth and immigration of low-skilled labor improves the efficiency of the labor market.

An Unequal Sharing of the Burden

A second issue with reducing low-skilled immigration relates to how fiscal burdens are shared across levels of government and across individuals. Whereas the federal government enjoys revenues from payroll taxes and income taxes generated by immigrants, states and localities tend to be responsible for funding K-12 education and public health care for the children of immigrants. The federal government thus enjoys more of the fiscal benefits of immigration while states and localities are stuck with a much higher share of the costs. Such inequities in burden sharing have provoked protest by governors in high-immigration states.

Another source of unequal burden sharing is that U.S. employers enjoy benefits from immigration, in terms of higher productivity for their operations, while taxpayers pay for the education and health services that immigrant households receive. Taxpayers thus subsidize employers in agriculture, construction, meatpacking, restaurants and hotels, and other sectors that have high levels of employment of low-skilled immigrant labor. A reasonable solution to the current predicament is to eliminate such subsidies by making employers internalize the fiscal cost of immigrant workers. One way of achieving internalization is to subject employers to an immigrant labor payroll tax that would fund the benefits that their immigrant employees, and their family members, receive. Such a tax would make employers bear the fiscal consequences of immigration, releasing taxpayers from the burden and perhaps easing political opposition to immigration.

Aligning Incentives, Sharing Gains

Immigration moves workers from countries where they are less productive to countries where they are more productive. Simply by crossing the U.S.-Mexico border, Mexican workers see their hourly wage increase by a factor of 2.5, adjusting for cost of living differences between the United States and Mexico. Students from Vietnam, Ghana, or Bolivia who obtain graduate degrees in the United States develop the potential to publish academic research or create patentable technology that they could not have accomplished at home. For the world as a whole, international migration appears to increase total income and generate large gains for those who take the risk of moving from one nation to another.

Convincing the American public that immigration benefits them, and not just migrants, is a task few politicians are willing to embrace. Yet, evidence suggests that for the United States immigration of high-skilled labor accelerates the rate of productivity growth and immigration of low-skilled labor improves the efficiency of the labor market. The downsides of immigration, brought about in part by the entry of undocumented workers, include adverse consequences for U.S. taxpayers. The problem is not immigration per se but rules governing taxes and spending that fail to make U.S. employers internalize the fiscal consequences of hiring low-skilled foreign labor. The nation could preserve the benefits from immigration and increase its public support by shifting the fiscal burden of immigration from taxpayers to employers. If we as a nation are going to continue to support immigration, we need to find arrangements that align the incentives of employers, households, and workers.

6

Open Borders Hurt US Workers

Michael Cutler

Michael Cutler is a retired senior agent with the Immigration and Naturalization Service, an organization whose functions are now divided among three agencies within the Department of Homeland Security. He is currently a senior analyst with Californians for Population Stabilization (CAPS), an organization that advocates policies to limit immigration.

One of the goals of strict immigration laws is to protect American workers from having to compete with illegal immigrants for jobs. Nevertheless, the Obama administration refuses to arrest and deport many of those who enter the United States illegally. Moreover, the administration mocks immigration law by authorizing the employment of illegal immigrants. In addition, some policy makers audaciously claim that "privileged" high-skilled American workers contribute to income inequality in the United States. Thus, they argue that the government should increase the number of high-skilled immigrants to reduce this inequality, a policy that is clearly anti-American.

In nearly all officially sanctioned endeavors that involve competition, referees or other such officials are employed to make certain that all competitors are given a "level playing field" to create a fair environment. In baseball, umpires provide this vital component to the integrity of the sport.

Society's Referees

Where government is concerned, laws and law enforcement officers are supposed to provide that same sort of fairness. Civil Rights laws have been enacted in the United States in an effort to provide equal treatment. In fact, the terms "just" and "fair" are often used in conjunction with one another. Among the duties of law enforcement officers is the role they are supposed to play as societal referees when they enforce the laws that are intended to protect lives and rights of those who live within their jurisdiction.

Today, competition can be found in many aspects of the lives of our citizens. Competition is especially keen where the search for jobs is concerned. Today many millions of American workers are either unemployed or underemployed. This has resulted in many Americans falling below the poverty line and many American families losing their homes to foreclosure because their "breadwinners" have lost their jobs.

The impact of this can be felt as it ripples throughout the economy of the United States where a glut of foreclosed houses have depressed real estate values in nearly every city and fewer Americans have the money to spend on nonessential items, thus creating a vicious downward cycle.

Preventing the Entry of Harmful Aliens

The immigration laws of the United States are supposed to prevent the entry and continued presence in the United States of aliens whose presence is harmful. Aliens who are engaged in criminal or terrorist activities are supposed to be prevented from entering the United States and removed (deported) from the United States when they [are] found present in the United States. Aliens who are convicted of committing felonies are also supposed to be deported from the United States when they complete serving their prison sentences.

Aliens who would seek unauthorized employment to be prevented from entering the United States . . . are supposed to be arrested [and] deported from the United States if such aliens succeed in entering the United States and seek employment. This is to prevent foreign workers from creating unfair and illegal competition for jobs Americans desperately need, especially in this era of economic hardship confronting all too many American workers and their families. This component of the immigration laws is nothing new. In fact, prior to the Second World War, the enforcement and administration of the immigration laws was the responsibility of the United States Department of Labor. Prior to World War II, where immigration was concerned, was the harm that unfettered immigration would do to American workers.

Today, in the wake of the terrorist attacks of September 11, 2001, and with increasing presence of transnational gangs and drug trafficking cartel members in the United States, America's borders have never been more important.

During the Second World War it became clear that the government needed to be concerned about the threats posed by aliens who would enter the United States to engage in espionage and acts of sabotage. On August 6, 2011, CAPS posted my commentary about the national security components of border security and immigration law enforcement.

Within the commentary I referenced an important article that appears on the FBI website about how, during WWII, the U.S. Coast Guard and the FBI worked cooperatively to thwart a Nazi plot to enable Nazi saboteurs to enter the United States to destroy factories that were producing weapons and other key products to assist the Allies.

The Importance of Securing America's Borders

Today, in the wake of the terrorist attacks of September 11, 2001, and with increasing presence of transnational gangs and drug trafficking cartel members in the United States, America's borders have never been more important and the failures to secure those borders and effectively enforce and administer the immigration laws have never been of greater importance, yet the current administration is failing at securing the borders and has done nothing to enhance the integrity to the system by which applications for immigration benefits and, in fact, has made an utter mockery of that entire system by providing employment authorization to potentially millions of illegal alien "DREAMERS. . . ."[1]

In addition to creating a national security nightmare by providing terrorists with an opportunity to game this program and acquire brand new "clean" identities, these failures are also creating unfair and illegal competition for American workers of every race, religion and ethnicity. Indeed, the unemployment and poverty rates are highest among American minorities!

American workers are not only facing unfair and illegal competition from illegal aliens who evade the inspections process but by aliens who successfully game the visa process.

On April 30, 2009, the U.S. Senate's Subcommittee on Immigration conducted a hearing on the topic: "Comprehensive Immigration Reform in 2009, Can We Do It and How?" Among the witnesses called to testify before that hearing was [economist and former Federal Reserve chairman] Alan Greenspan, arguably one of the key architects of the economic crisis, who stated:

1. The author refers to the DREAM Act, in which illegal immigrants who arrived before they were sixteen years old are allowed to apply for permanent resident status. They must have lived in the United States for five consecutive years, have served in the US military if they are men, have graduated from high school, and be of good moral character.

... The second bonus (in accelerating the influx of skilled immigrant workers) would address the increasing concentration of income in this country. Greatly expanding our quotas for the highly skilled would lower wage premiums of skilled over lesser skilled. Skill shortages in America exist because we are shielding our skilled labor force from world competition. Quotas have been substituted for the wage pricing mechanism. In the process, we have created a privileged elite whose incomes are being supported at non-competitively high levels by immigration quotas on skilled professionals. Eliminating such restrictions would reduce at least some of our income inequality.

Clearly Greenspan demonstrated unmitigated chutzpah, referring to skilled Americans as the "privileged elite!" His infuriating goal of reducing skill-based income inequality is nothing short of anti-American in both ways of interpreting that statement. It flies in the face of the American dream and would serve to pull the floor out from under American middle class workers and their families!

When the fans watching a baseball game disagree with the call of an umpire they are likely to yell, "Throw the bum out!"

Think of that simple, yet direct four word phrase on Election Day if you determine that the candidate for office for whom you are voting has failed to be fair to American workers and their families.

7

Open Borders Enrich the United States

Darrell M. West

Darrell M. West, vice president of governance studies and director of the Center for Technology Innovation at the Brookings Institution, is author of Brain Gain: Rethinking U.S. Immigration Policy.

The benefits of policies that open US borders to immigrants far outweigh the costs. In fact, founders of several American high tech companies came to the United States as students and started their business after they graduated. In addition, as many as two-thirds of Americans believe that immigrants have improved US culture. Indeed, one study reveals that diverse communities are more creative and productive. The United States has imported talented immigrant directors, actors, and sports stars that enrich the nation. Rather than focus on unwarranted fears about competition for jobs or depressed earnings, US immigration policies should focus on immigrants as valuable American assets.

Few things are more controversial than immigration. The flood of illegal immigrants across U.S. borders enrages many native-born residents. People worry that immigrants compete for jobs, unfairly draw on government benefits, and fundamentally alter the social fabric of America. They fear

Darrell M. West, "The Costs and Benefits of Immigration," *Political Science Quarterly*, vol. 126, no. 3, Fall 2011, pp. 427–428, 437–442. Copyright © 2011 by The Brookings Institution. All rights reserved. Reproduced by permission.

that our culture is losing its distinctive character due to non-English-speaking foreigners who move to the United States and do not integrate into mainstream social and political life.

Explaining Immigration Fears

Part of this anxiety is rooted in ethnocentrism and group animus. Citizens do not like immigrants who look or act differently from themselves. As Donald Kinder and Cindy Kam have noted in their recent book, ethnocentrism is common in a number of different societies. People divide themselves into "in-groups" and "out-groups" and these types of "us versus them" distinctions color public opinion and make it difficult to develop balanced public policies.

Other observers are concerned about immigration because they view the material costs of open-door policies as broad-based, while the benefits are concentrated. As argued by researcher Gary Freeman, the impact of open policies falls on disadvantaged workers who feel their wages are depressed by newcomers and on taxpayers who worry about a drain on public resources, while the benefits accrue to small groups of successful immigrants who get good jobs and some businesses that gain the skills of new arrivals.

Skilled immigrants clearly have been a big part of the rise of the high-tech and biotech industries.

Both ideas (group animosity and unfavorable costs/benefits) make it virtually impossible for our political system to resolve this conflict. Many taxpayers feel that immigrants receive more benefits than they warrant and that the social costs of undocumented arrivals are enormous. As long as these are the prevailing citizen interpretations, immigration will remain controversial, many will favor punitive policies, and it will prove impossible for political leaders to address this topic.

In this article, I seek to reframe the public debate over immigration policy by arguing that the benefits of immigration are much broader than popularly imagined and the costs are more confined. In spite of legitimate fear and anxiety over illegal immigration, I suggest that immigrants bring a "brain gain" of innovation and creativity that outweighs real or imagined costs. Immigrants have enriched our economic, intellectual, social, and cultural life in a number of fundamental respects. We need a new national narrative on immigration that moves from themes of "illegality and abuse" to those of "innovation and enrichment.". . .

High-Tech Development

Skilled immigrants clearly have been a big part of the rise of the high-tech and biotech industries. One study of technology and engineering businesses launched in America between 1995 to 2005 found that 25.3 percent had a foreign-born founder. In California, this percentage was even higher at 38.8 percent. And in Silicon Valley, famed home of high-tech industry, 52.4 percent of new-tech startups had a foreign-born owner. According to its count, "immigrant-founded companies produced $52 billion in sales and employed 450,000 workers in 2005."

This report found that nearly a quarter of the international patents filed from the United States in 2006 were based on the work of foreign-borns living in America. In comparing innovation from 1998 to 2006, the percentage of foreign-born patents rose from 7.3 to 24.2. Consistent with a "brain gain" hypothesis, many of these founders were well-educated, held degrees in science, technology, engineering, and math, and were educated at American universities. Fifty-three percent of them had their highest degree with a U.S. university, suggesting that there is great value in bringing the foreign born to America, educating them, and keeping them here in U.S. jobs.

Gnanaraj Chellaraj, Keith Maskus, and Aaditya Mattoo estimate the impact of immigration on patent applications and awards. They find that international graduate students and skilled immigrants have a positive impact on patent generation. Their figures demonstrate that increasing "the number of foreign graduate students would raise patent applications by 4.7 percent, university patent grants by 5.3 percent and non-university patent grants by 6.7 percent."

Immigrants over the last decade have displayed a high level of entrepreneurial spirit.

Indeed, most high-tech founders who came to America from abroad did so as students and then started business careers after graduation. Foreign students are highly motivated individuals who come to the United States for education, and then would like to get jobs, launch businesses, and develop innovative ideas. They are a source of great talent and an engine of economic development.

According to the Kauffman Index of Entrepreneurial Activity, immigrants over the last decade have displayed a high level of entrepreneurial spirit. If one breaks down entrepreneurial activities between immigrants and native-borns for the years 1996 through 2008, immigrants consistently demonstrate greater entrepreneurship than native-borns. They are twice as likely to start new businesses. In 2008, for example, 0.53 percent of immigrants launched a business, compared to 0.28 percent of native-born individuals.

Policies That Encouraged Talented Immigrants

AnnaLee Saxenian traces the rise of America's high-tech boom to Congressional passage of the Immigration Act of 1965 (also known as the Hart-Cellar Act). Dating back to the Johnson-Reed Immigration Act of 1924, the United States imposed strict limits on immigration from specific countries. For example, Taiwan and many other Asian nations were limited to 100 immigrants per year, which placed a tight cap on Asian scientists and engineers. The Hart-Cellar Act started Asia's brain drain by creating opportunities for foreigners with special skills to migrate to America. Later legislation such as the Immigration and Nationality Act of 1990 expanded these opportunities by boosting visas based on technical talent from 54,000 to 140,000.

According to Saxenian, it is no coincidence that the high-tech boom began when Asian scientists and engineers came to the United States in large numbers. Silicon Valley started to attract Chinese and Indian talent immediately after 1965. Based on her research, there were 92,020 Chinese and 28,520 Indians in the Silicon Valley workforce by 1990 and "84 percent of the Chinese and 98 percent of the Indians were immigrants." These numbers grew even larger in the 1990s and early twenty-first century.

The number of foreign students admitted to American science and engineering graduate programs also rose during this time period. With the help of federal financial aid programs and increases in research and development funding, American universities grew substantially and expanded the size of their PhD programs. From 1960 to 2000, the raw number of international students increased eightfold. During this period, America went from 23 percent of PhD awardees in 1966 being foreign-born to 39 percent in 2000.

Innovative Immigrants

A national survey asked Americans whether they believe immigration improved U.S. culture with new ideas and customs. More than two thirds of Americans (68 percent) said they thought immigrants improved U.S. culture through new ideas. This provides perceptual support for the argument that immigrants add value, diversity, and ideas to civic life.

Individuals such as Sergey Brin have made major contributions to business and intellectual life. Brin is the founder of the path-breaking search engine firm Google. He was born in Moscow, Russia, and moved to the United States at the age of six. His parents were mathematicians and he quickly developed an aptitude for math and computer science. At Stanford University, he met classmate Larry Page and the two combined their respective interests in data mining and search efficiency to form the now legendary and highly successful company Google, Inc.

Immigrants have made dramatic contributions to science and technology.

This corporation revolutionized computing by developing a very efficient Internet search engine. As the Web grew in size and complexity, having good search features became essential to maximizing information usage. Search represented a way for people to tame the information flow and find the material they needed. It put people in charge of information, as opposed to the other way around. This innovation allowed the Internet to thrive and develop, and people turned to it for business, education, and health care.

Pierre Omidyar displayed a similar ingenuity. Born in Paris, France, in 1967 of Iranian parents, he came to America as a young child. With an interest in computers, he earned a degree in computer science from Tufts University and served as a software developer for several computer companies. After working on an Internet shopping site, he designed an online auction service that he called Auction Web in 1995. On this site, people could request bids for collectibles, and items were sold to the highest bidder. Two years later, he renamed the company eBay and soon had over one million customers. By 2003, the business had grown to 95 million registered users, had sales of over $2 billion, and was expanding into India and China.

The company transformed commerce by allowing for direct sales people-to-people. Consistent with the digital era, he empowered ordinary folks and cut out the middle-men in business transactions. That allowed markets in niche areas to flourish and the company to connect buyers and sellers. His leadership paved the way for other Internet companies to thrive in various niches.

Immigrants have made dramatic contributions to science and technology. Andy Grove is one of the leaders in the areas of semiconductors and microchips. Born in Budapest, Hungary, Grove migrated to the United States and wrote leading papers on semiconductors. He founded the Intel Corporation in 1968 and made it the leading company in the field. As microchips got smaller and smaller, computers got cheaper and more powerful. The computing era would not have thrived to the extent it did without his leadership.

Jerry Wang represents another example of an immigrant visionary. Born in Taiwan, he came to America when he was 10 years old. In college, his hobby was compiling links of favorite websites into a central service. This later formed the nucleus of his company, Yahoo. The firm eventually became a successful portal that offered news, entertainment, search, email, and social networking. It is estimated that nearly 500 million people around the world use his company's email service.

Cities that have diverse and creative residents tend to be more pleasant and productive places.

The Social Costs and Benefits

As challenging as is the computation of immigration's economic and intellectual contributions, the social costs and benefits are harder to measure. Because they involve less-tangible ramifications than taxes, employment, government benefits, or patents, it is more challenging to estimate the actual magnitude of social contributions. We intuitively understand there is immigrant value in food, the arts, culture, and athletics, but it is difficult to determine them precisely.

Researchers Gianmarco Ottaviano and Giovanni Peri have attempted to evaluate the value of cultural diversity in the United States. They asked who can deny the value of "Italian restaurants, French beauty shops, German breweries, Belgian cholcolate stores, Russian ballets, Chinese markets, and Indian tea houses." Through the globalization of food, culture, and artistic expression, metropolitan areas with greater diversity show higher wages. According to Ottaviano and Peri, American workers benefit from this because "a more multicultural urban environment makes US-born citizens more productive."

Richard Florida has taken this argument one step further by suggesting a correlation between geographic diversity, innovation, and productivity. Cities that have diverse and creative residents tend to be more pleasant and productive places. People like to live in these cities, and this increases innovation, home prices, the local economy, and civic pride.

A 2007 Gallup Poll sought to get a handle on this subject by asking how immigrants had affected "food, music, and the arts" in America. Forty percent indicated that immigrants had made things better, 9 percent felt they had made them worse, and 46 percent concluded there had not been much of an effect. Not surprisingly, there were substantial differences by race and ethnicity. Sixty-five percent of Hispanics felt immigrants had improved food, music, and the arts, compared to 34 percent of African-Americans, and 37 percent of whites.

The Cultural Contributions of Immigrants

The internationalization of arts and culture has led to an influx of talented directors and performers from abroad. Of Hollywood directors who received multiple Academy Awards, nine of the 17 were foreign born. Individuals such as Salma

Hayek, Mikhail Baryshnikov, Jim Carrey, and Dan Aykroyd enriched the world of television, dancing, and film. Hayek is a Mexican-born actress who came to America for boarding school when she was 12 years old. She went on to leading roles in movies such as *Frida, Mi Vida Loca*, and *Wild Wild West*.

The same argument holds for sports. It is hard to imagine contemporary American baseball without immigration. Baseball is a sport that used to be played by white Americans, then was integrated by African Americans and American Hispanics, and now is populated by athletes from Japan, the Dominican Republic, Cuba, Jamaica, and Venezuela. Sammy Sosa, from the Dominican Republic, became one of the leading home-run hitters in major league history. In recent years, 29 percent of the players in major league baseball were born outside the United States, mainly in the Dominican Republic or Venezuela.

Immigrants contribute to the vibrancy of our economic development and the richness of our cultural life.

Education and philanthropy have benefitted from foreign émigrés. As an example, Vartan Gregorian was born in Tabiz, Iran, of Armenian heritage and became a leader in the fields of higher education and philanthropy. Educated in Lebanon, he moved to America in 1956. He served as provost at the University of Pennsylvania, president of the New York Public Library, president of Brown University, and president of the Carnegie Corporation of New York, one of the leading philanthropic foundations in America. As a leading educator, author, and professor, he brought a strong sense of innovation to higher-education and the world of philanthropy. He showed leading institutions how to improve the plight of the disadvantaged and make an impact on those passing through their doors.

The Policy Ramifications

In the end, the central question for immigration policy is the balance between costs and benefits. Vivek Wadhwa and colleagues reach a clear conclusion based on their studies. They say that "immigrants have become a significant driving force in the creation of new businesses and intellectual property in the U.S., and their contributions have increased over the past decade."

Unlike the view of critics who worry about job competition or depressed earnings from foreigners, there is considerable research suggesting that immigrants contribute to the vibrancy of our economic development and the richness of our cultural life. They start new businesses, patent novel ideas, and create jobs. Americans need to reconceptualize immigration as a brain gain for the United States.

We need to do this in a manner that does not produce class, racial, or ethnic biases. The smart child from a low Indian caste deserves the same consideration as a white engineer from the United Kingdom. We should seek smart, creative, and innovative individuals from Asia, Africa, and Latin America, not just Europe. We should recognize that poor and working-class students often are highly motivated, and therefore deserving of consideration for entry into the United States. Our national policy needs to recognize the past contributions that newcomers have made and facilitate the arrival of other immigrants who will bring equally important assets to the United States.

8

The US Should Provide Better Evidence That Its Borders Are Secure

Edward Alden and Bryan Roberts

Edward Alden is Bernard L. Schwartz Senior Fellow at the Council on Foreign Relations, a think tank whose goal is to shape foreign policy. Bryan Roberts is senior economist at Nathan Associates and a former assistant director in the Office of Program Analysis and Evaluation at the US Department of Homeland Security.

Rather than speculate on the effectiveness of border security policies, policy makers should develop ways to measure their efficacy. Although the number of border arrests has, in fact, declined, no evidence reveals why. Apprehension rates provide only a partial picture. In fact, many analysts contend that enhanced enforcement provides little deterrent. The question of whether border patrol security is adequate cannot be effectively answered unless data demonstrates what actually deters immigrants from crossing in the first place or from trying to do so again, once they have been apprehended. Only when officials get an adequate answer to this question can the United States implement effective border security policies.

In response to record numbers of illegal border crossings and the security fears triggered by the 9/11 attacks, over the past two decades the United States has steadily increased its efforts to secure its borders against illegal immigration. The number of U.S. Border Patrol agents has risen from fewer than 3,000 to more than 20,700; nearly 700 miles of fencing have been built along the southern border with Mexico; and surveillance systems, including pilotless drones, now monitor much of the rest of the border. In a speech in El Paso, Texas, in May [2011], U.S. President Barack Obama claimed that the United States had "strengthened border security beyond what many believed was possible." Yet according to a Fox News poll taken last year [2010], nearly three-quarters of Americans think the border is no more, or even less, secure than it was five years ago. Some administration critics claim that the United States' frontiers have never been more porous.

This contradiction stems in part from the fact that the Department of Homeland Security (DHS) has never clearly defined what border control means in practice. A secure border cannot mean one with no illegal crossings—that would be unrealistic for almost any country, especially one as big and as open as the United States. On the other hand, the borders cannot be considered secure if many of those attempting to enter illegally succeed. Defining a sensible middle ground, where border enforcement and other programs discourage many illegal crossings and most of those who try to cross illegally are apprehended, is the challenge.

The Obama administration must develop effective ways to measure progress on border security and then inform Congress and the public regularly about it.

A Failure to Measure Border Security Success

Unfortunately, the U.S. government has failed to develop good measures for fixing goals and determining progress toward them. Since 2005, the DHS has reported how many miles of the country's land borders are under its "operational control," but it has done so without having clearly defined what that standard means and without providing hard data to back it up. The lack of sound measurement has left the administration touting its efforts rather than their results: during a press conference in 2010, Obama noted, "We have more of everything: ICE [Immigration and Customs Enforcement], Border Patrol, surveillance, you name it. So we take border security seriously."

It is no wonder, then, that many critics dispute the president's claims. In Congress, the result has been a stalemate over border policy that has stymied progress on every other aspect of immigration reform. Obama's opponents, led by longtime supporters of immigration reform, including Republican Senators John McCain, Lindsey Graham, and Jon Kyl, have demanded that the borders be secured before any other aspect of immigration reform is addressed. Last year, for example, Congress approved almost unanimously an additional $600 million for border enforcement, on top of the $17 billion annual budget. But every other immigration proposal—including the DREAM Act, a bill that would grant residency to the children of illegal immigrants who attend a U.S. college for two years or join the military; new programs for temporary agricultural workers; and increased quotas for high-skilled immigrants—has been held up because of congressional demands that the border be secured first.

To move the debate on border security beyond politically driven speculation to a more serious consideration of how much enforcement is needed, and at what cost, the Obama administration must develop effective ways to measure progress on border security and then inform Congress and the public regularly about it.

Measuring Apprehensions

For most of its history, the United States has known little about the people who attempt to cross its borders illegally. Beyond its yearly count of apprehensions, most of which occur along the U.S.-Mexican border, the Border Patrol reports very little data to the public. In 1986, the agency recorded the largest annual number of arrests—1,693,000—as immigrants flooded to the border hoping to take advantage of a new immigration bill that offered legal residency to many who were already illegally in the United States. In 2000, the number of arrests was almost as high, driven by the strong U.S. economy and rising numbers of young workers looking for higher wages in the United States. Arrests have dropped sharply since then. Only 463,000 were made in 2010, the lowest number since 1972.

On its own, the number of apprehensions gives only a hazy picture of the number of immigrants actually trying to sneak across the border, since a given individual may be caught multiple times or may enter without ever being caught. Moreover, arrest figures can highlight patterns of illegal immigration but cannot explain why they change. In the early 1990s, for example, Border Patrol arrests near the Californian-Mexican border averaged nearly 600,000 annually. After the government strengthened enforcement there in the mid-1990s, apprehensions fell by half in California but soared in Arizona, indicating that the illegal traffic had merely shifted east. (Today, Arizona remains the largest illegal-entry corridor into the United States. This helps explain the political backlash against immigration that led to the state's 2010 adoption of the controversial law known as SB 1070, which increases the state police's powers to arrest suspected illegal immigrants.) Without data to supplement annual arrest figures, it is hard to say whether the past decade's falling apprehension numbers are a victory for enforcement or simply the result of a weaker U.S. economy that is no longer a magnet for immigrant workers. For its part, the DHS claims that effective enforcement explains the recent drop in the number of apprehensions. Yet a decade ago, the DHS' predecessor agency, the Immigration and Naturalization Service, claimed that better enforcement accounted for the peak in the arrest numbers. A measure that indicates success whether it rises or falls is not very useful without further information.

Patrolling for Data

On its Web site, the Border Patrol states that "although the Border Patrol has changed dramatically since its inception over 80 years ago, its overall mission remains unchanged: to detect and prevent illegal entry of aliens into the United States." Currently, the DHS claims that nearly 900 out of the 1,969 miles of the U.S.-Mexican border are under the Border Patrol's control, but it has not presented hard data to support that claim. A good place to start is estimating apprehension rates, that is, the number of arrests compared to total illegal crossings. With all the manpower, fencing, and surveillance that have been deployed along the U.S.-Mexican border, one would expect the U.S. government to be catching a higher percentage of illegal immigrants today than ever before. But the government currently does not report that rate.

Although a high apprehension rate is a positive indicator, it is still insufficient as a measure of success.

Reasonable estimates can certainly be compiled. Since 1997, the Border Patrol has made internal calculations of "known illegal entries." The numbers come from close observation conducted by individual agents, who collect information about footprints and other physical evidence of human traffic across the U.S.-Mexican border, and from images from surveillance cameras. However, these Border Patrol estimates are rarely cited publicly, and when they are, they are used in a highly selective fashion. For example, a recent Government Accountability Office report stated that 90 percent of known illegal entrants in one sector, in Yuma, Arizona, were either apprehended or deterred from entering in 2009. But Yuma has seen a huge enforcement buildup in recent years, so very few immigrants attempt to cross there.

To be sure, this measure is almost certainly higher than the true apprehension rate, since known illegal entrants do not include those who successfully cross unnoticed. In contrast, another component of the DHS, the U.S. Coast Guard, has been calculating and reporting an apprehension rate based on known illegal entries at sea since the mid-1990s. It estimates that the apprehension rate at sea is about 60 percent.

Trying to Explain Varying Apprehension Rates

Academic studies have also offered estimates of the apprehension rate. In 1994, Thomas Espenshade of Princeton's Office of Population Research developed a model that uses fingerprint data to identify individuals that the Border Patrol has caught trying to sneak across the border more than once. According to his research, evidence from those caught multiple times can be used to estimate with some accuracy the likelihood that an immigrant will be arrested on any given trip to the United States. He concluded that between 1977 and 1988, when there were only one-sixth as many Border Patrol agents as there are today, the apprehension rate was about 30 percent. This finding echoes studies by Princeton University's Mexican Migration Project, which since the 1980s has surveyed households in Mexican towns that have high emigration rates. They, too, suggest that the apprehension rate of those trying to cross illegally into the United States was around 30 percent between 1965 and 2005. Recent data from surveys of immigrants suggest that the rate may have risen in recent years.

If the estimates based on known illegal entries are too high, these are almost certainly too low, because they do not take into account immigrants who give up trying to cross after being caught. Taking deterrence into account, the true apprehension rate today for the entire southwestern border is likely between 40 and 50 percent, and it may have risen in recent years due to increased enforcement resources. The DHS is reluctant to publish a figure, however, probably because it varies greatly among different border sectors and because the data are better for some sectors than others. Although a high apprehension rate is a positive indicator, it is still insufficient as a measure of success. As with all law enforcement, the real aim of border enforcement is to deter illegal acts. Effective enforcement is impossible if lawbreaking is the norm. Even a very high apprehension rate would be less than desirable if many people kept trying.

Without clearer models of illegal immigration, the [Obama] administration cannot isolate the role of enforcement.

Keeping Illegal Immigrants at Home

There are two types of deterrence relevant to border security: behind-the-border deterrence, in which enforcement discourages would-be immigrants from ever trying to cross illegally, and at-the-border deterrence, in which those who have been caught crossing the border at least once are deterred from trying to do so again. In an ideal system, the first kind of deterrence would work well enough to obviate the need for the second kind. Assessing behind-the-border deterrence is difficult, however, since it requires information about both people who decided to immigrate illegally and those who decided not to for fear of being caught.

The long-standing consensus of most academic research on illegal immigration, from such respected scholars as Douglas Massey of Princeton University and Wayne Cornelius of the University of California, San Diego, is that enforcement has little behind-the-border deterrent effect. Instead, this re-search argues that attempted entries are largely driven by eco-nomics; when the U.S. economy is strong, especially in sectors that employ many illegal immigrants, such as construction, the numbers rise. This has certainly been the historical pat-tern: total apprehension figures dropped during the recessions of 1981–82, 1990–91, and 2001–2.

Yet there is some evidence that deterrence is growing. The latest decline in apprehensions began well before the 2008 re-cession and has yet to be reversed, even as the U.S. economy is recovering. But without clearer models of illegal immigration, the administration cannot isolate the role of enforcement. The number of illegal crossings will likely rise again as the U.S. economy continues to recover, but since the current metrics are so poor, it will be impossible to tell whether that increase should be attributed to better economic conditions in the United States or to deficiencies in border security. At the mo-ment, the only available measure of at-the-border deterrence— from surveys of Mexican immigrants—is discouraging. It sug-gests that in the last decade, 90–98 percent of the Mexican nationals who tried to enter the United States illegally were ultimately successful. The odds of apprehension on any given journey have likely increased, but persistence continues to pay off. This appears to be due to the involvement of professional smugglers. Evidence suggests that half of all illegal crossers hired smugglers in the 1970s and that this proportion has risen significantly since. Data on the average fee paid to smug-glers, which are collected by the immigrant surveys, show that, adjusted for inflation, the fee doubled between the early 1990s and 2005. In part, these increasing fees may explain both the apparent increase in behind-the-border deterrence and the minimal effectiveness of at-the-border deterrence: some im-migrants cannot afford smugglers, so they stay at home, and those who decide to pay a smuggler are determined to try un-til they succeed. (Immigrants typically pay smugglers half the fee in advance and half on their successful entry, so smugglers will guide the immigrants on multiple attempts.) Smuggling plays a critical role in facilitating illegal entry into the United States, and the DHS needs to collect, analyze, and report data on smuggling operations more systematically.

The Border Patrol has long recognized the importance of deterrence at the border. But for decades, it simply returned most of the Mexican immigrants it apprehended to just over the border, only to see them try to cross again and again. It has recently begun imposing penalties, such as jail time or a flight to the interior of Mexico. There is not yet good data, however, on whether these new methods are increasing deterrence. If the goal of border enforcement is to prevent successful illegal entry into the United States, the government will need to devise better ways to track those who overstay their visas or are smuggled in through legal ports of entry. Ultimately, the U.S. government needs to generate reasonably accurate measures of the total inflow of illegal immigrants in order to develop the most effective policy responses. Measuring illegal immigration may seem inherently difficult, but in 2000 and 2001, the government explicitly set the twin goals of reducing both illegal immigrant inflows and the total number of unauthorized immigrants in the United States. And those numbers are routinely estimated by experts both inside and outside the government. After the DHS was formed in 2002, the regular measuring of progress toward these goals stopped, but it is clear that taking such measurements is possible if the political will exists.

Why Metrics Matter

Systematically reported apprehension rates and deterrence data would give Congress better information to decide whether the money spent on border security is wisely allocated. Border security budgets have ballooned over the past decade, but the results are unclear. Right now, questions about whether current spending is adequate to control the border and, if not, how much would be are largely unanswerable. With better measures, the government could experiment with new programs. For example, increased numbers of legal work opportunities would likely reduce incentives to cross illegally. But unless Congress had some confidence that this could be measured and verified, it would be reluctant to authorize the program. If the government could better track illegal crossings, it could test pilot programs of new initiatives as an intermediate step.

Similarly, improved measurement could help determine the relative effectiveness of various enforcement tools. The DHS has no real understanding of how much border control improves when the number of Border Patrol agents, sensors, or miles of fencing increases. It also has no understanding of the relative effectiveness of border enforcement as compared to efforts to prevent employers from hiring illegal workers. Signs that the DHS and Congress are finally starting to seek more reliable border security metrics are mixed. At a February 2011 hearing before the House Homeland Security Subcommittee on Border and Maritime Security, Michael Fisher, the Border Patrol chief, noted that "operational control is not in and of itself an assessment of border security." The Border Patrol has said that the agency is working on a new set of performance metrics that will improve the assessment of border security. However, at a hearing in May, DHS Secretary Janet Napolitano instead promised new measures of success focused on "overall security and quality of life along the entire border region." Such assessments would miss the point: it would be as if local police forces measured property values rather than crime rates. Better border enforcement will certainly improve the quality of life along the border, but that is a consequence of a job well done, not the job itself. The DHS needs to develop and report measures that directly address its mission, and the government will need to establish clear targets and genuine metrics for progress. Without them, the policy debate will remain mired in unfounded claims and immeasurable goals.

9

Measures to Secure the Canadian Border Hinder Relations with Canada

Jena Baker McNeill and Diem Nguyen

Jena Baker McNeill is a policy analyst on issues of homeland security, and Diem Nguyen is a research assistant in the Douglas and Sarah Allison Center for Foreign Policy Studies at The Heritage Foundation, a conservative public policy think tank.

Policies designed to secure the US-Canadian border should recognize the United States' long-standing and productive relationship with Canada. Both nations are significant partners in trade and tourism. Moreover, Canada has always been one of America's staunchest allies. Since securing the 5,525-mile border is costly, the United States and Canada should encourage private-sector involvement to fill security gaps. In truth, more productive policies such as antiterrorism information sharing and combined law enforcement efforts will better protect the security of both nations.

On January 15, [2009] the United States Northern Command Joint Task Force-North accidentally released to the public a briefing that expressed concerns over terrorists entering the U.S. from Canada. While the report was taken offline and out of public view shortly thereafter, this briefing is one of many reports centered on U.S./Canadian security policies,

Jena Baker McNeill and Diem Nguyen, *U.S., Canada Working Together on Improving Border Security*, The Heritage Foundation Web Memo No. 2239, March 6, 2009. Copyright © 2009 by The Heritage Foundation. All rights reserved. Reproduced by permission.

including a recent request by Homeland Security Secretary Janet Napolitano for information relating to the mechanisms and programs currently in place at the U.S. northern border.

While the recommendations of the U.S. Northern Command briefing were not made public, the recent focus on the northern border has left many citizens from both countries concerned that the U.S. might decide to increase security measures at the border in a way that would hamper trade and travel. Initiatives to secure the United States from potential terrorists in Canada should extend beyond the border and center on information-sharing and other kinds of anti-terrorism cooperation, instituting processes and programs that respect both nations' sovereignty, and addresses common concerns—without hindering either nation's economic viability.

Economic Reliance

The U.S. Northern Command briefing cited Canada as a "favorable" environment for potential terrorists entering the U.S. due to the Canadian immigration policies toward aliens from Pakistan, Afghanistan, and Egypt. The briefing specifically cited the Great Lakes region of Canada and areas north of New York, Vermont, and New Hampshire as the areas of most concern and indicated that terrorists could be forming networks out of these regions.

> *The U.S. should look to "beyond the border" solutions— solutions that stop terrorists from entering North America altogether—and work together with Canada to arrest individuals engaged in plotting against either country.*

The Department of Homeland Security (DHS) created the Western Hemisphere Travel Initiative (WHTI) in 2004 to increase security on the northern border. This initiative requires proof of identity and citizenship for people crossing the border into the United States. But unfortunately, WHTI has significantly increased wait times at border crossing, delays which have been particularly damaging to those business that rely on the "just in time" process—that is, delivering products (such as fresh produce) just before they are made available for purchase.

This new briefing might well tempt Congress or DHS to institute similar or more aggressive security measures at the border; but this is not the right path for the following reasons:

- *Trade and travel*: Canada is the United States' biggest trading partner. Every day approximately $1.5 billion in goods and 300,000 people cross the northern border. Adding new security measures at the border without hurting the two economies would be extremely difficult.

- *U.S.-Canadian relations*: Canada is one of America's best allies. Canada's support in Afghanistan is one of the many illustrations of its committed friendship with the United States. Hardening the border would signal mistrust between these longtime allies and place a strain on the future of the American-Canadian relationship.

- *Cost*: The Canadian border is large, spanning 5,525 miles. It would cost the U.S. government a tremendous amount of resources to successfully secure the physical border. Given the economic (not to mention public diplomacy) consequences associated with such an effort, the U.S. should not spend precious resources in this manner.

Beyond the Physical Border

The U.S. should look to "beyond the border" solutions—solutions that stop terrorists from entering North America altogether—and work together with Canada to arrest individuals engaged in plotting against either country. DHS and Congress should:

- *Promote anti-terrorism information sharing.* Information sharing is the most effective way of tracking down dangerous people and protecting the country from attack. Information on a variety of things, such as criminal databases and customs information, should be shared between the two countries to enhance their anti-terrorism capabilities and to arrest those who seek to do harm.

- *Expand cross-border law enforcement programs.* Working together on law enforcement initiatives will make each country's homeland security much more efficient. Law enforcement can often disrupt terrorist activity before it starts, and improving cooperation in this area will bear fruit on both sides of the border. A great example of this kind of program is the Integrated Border Enforcement Team, a joint program that targets dangerous people and goods by sharing intelligence and law enforcement capabilities from various agencies. Similar cooperation efforts should be used for security missions.

- *Coordinate visa policies.* For example, U.S. and Canada should offer visa waiver status for the same list of countries. Coordinated visa policies will ensure that both countries institute similar security mechanisms in a way that is in compliance with America's security standards.

- *Encourage private investment in infrastructure.* Inadequate infrastructure at the border further jeopardizes security. The U.S. should find ways to encourage the private sector to invest in infrastructure (such as toll bridges) at the northern border. This will not only speed the processing of goods and services but will ensure that terrorists are not sneaking through because of gaps in ailing infrastructure. One way this can be accomplished is through the SAFETY Act, which provides liability protection for companies developing homeland security technologies. This protection is only for companies in the United States and greatly limits the deployment of these necessary technologies. By encouraging similar protections in Canada, DHS can help spur innovation and private investment in infrastructure at the border.

Good Neighbors

It is in the interest of both nations to keep terrorists out of North America. Working together, the U.S. and Canada can tackle security loopholes to ensure the security of Americans and Canadians alike while, at the same time, not disrupting economic ties or jeopardizing their close friendship.

10

Expanded Border Enforcement Strategies Have Reduced Illegal Immigration

Marshall Fitz

Marshall Fitz is director of immigration policy at the Center for American Progress, a progressive research and advocacy organization.

Enhanced border security manpower and fencing have reduced the number of illegal immigrants entering the United States. Apprehensions in each of the nine sectors, from San Diego to the Rio Grande Valley in Texas, have dropped significantly. Enhanced border security in the San Diego sector did in fact divert the flow of illegal immigration to other sectors, but as enhancements progressed across the southern border the flow slowed in all sectors, suggesting that the enhancements are a significant deterrent to illegal crossing. Unfortunately, increased border security has forced some to risk crossing in dangerous terrain or to resort to smugglers sponsored by drug cartels. Thus, in addition to enhanced border security, policy makers must develop immigration polices that facilitate beneficial immigration while halting illegal immigration that contributes to the drug trade.

A recent trip by this author and several colleagues to study the Arizona border was eye-opening. Not because we encountered scores of headless bodies, but because the border

Marshall Fitz, "Safer than Ever," Center for American Progress, August 2011. Copyright © 2011 by the Center for American Progress. All rights reserved. Reproduced by permission.

landscape has changed so dramatically in the last five years both literally and figuratively. Hundreds of miles of severe fencing, vehicle barriers, radio towers, flood lighting, and access roads have degraded the border's aesthetics and environmental quality. But in conjunction with surges in manpower and technology, this added infrastructure has also undeniably and fundamentally enhanced the Border Patrol's ability to prevent and intercept unauthorized migrants and smugglers.

All the recent statistics tell us that illegal immigration flows at our southern border have slowed dramatically. Numbers tell us that we no longer have a border across which thousands of people traverse illegally every day without our knowledge. Instead we have a border where the vast majority of attempted entries are identified and a far larger percentage of entrants are apprehended than ever before. Moreover, recent reports persuasively demonstrate that violent crime rates along the U.S.-Mexico border have been falling for years and that border cities of all sizes have maintained crime rates below the national average. . . .

A Dramatic Decline in Unlawful Entries

The Border Patrol has divided the 2,000-mile-long land border between the United States and Mexico into nine sectors. From west to east, they are: San Diego, El Centro, Yuma, Tucson, El Paso, Marfa, Del Rio, Laredo, and Rio Grande Valley. Analyzing the number of apprehensions sector by sector over time shows how the massive investments in manpower and infrastructure have altered migration flows while highlighting the challenges that remain. Border Patrol apprehensions in the San Diego sector, for example, were more than 565,000 in 1992. By 2000, with significant fencing in place and increased manpower, that number had dropped to 151,000. But as those numbers dropped over time, the flow didn't stop; it just shifted east into the El Centro, Yuma, and Tucson border sectors.

Crossings in the El Centro and Yuma sectors had been less frequent because they have more remote and inhospitable terrain and are further from easy access and transit to employment opportunities. In 1992 border apprehensions in the El Centro sector were around 30,000, around 25,000 in Yuma, and about 71,000 in Tucson. Increased enforcement efforts in the San Diego sector, however, displaced the flow from that area and created a huge spike in entries and apprehensions in those more remote sectors. By 2000 El Centro apprehensions were more than 238,000, Yuma apprehensions at nearly 110,000, and Tucson became the main corridor, reaching a peak of more than 616,000.

Massive new infusions of border enforcement resources added to the effort since 2000 put the squeeze on the El Centro and Yuma sectors of the border. By FY 2010 the number of apprehensions in El Centro had dropped back to around 32,000 and Yuma apprehensions had fallen to an incredibly low 7,100.

Only the Tucson sector remains a challenge. The number of apprehensions dropped by more than 400,000 between 2000 and 2010 but they were still at 212,000.

The decrease in apprehensions reflects a dramatic downturn in attempted entries, and, what's more, the percentage *of individuals apprehended is way up.*

Redirecting the Flow of Illegal Crossings

One might ask: Have the efforts in El Centro, Yuma, and Tucson reverted some of the flows to San Diego? The answer is no. San Diego apprehensions have continued to decline and fell to a little more than 68,000 in 2010. Why? Because the infrastructure there is mature and the deterrent effect has been profound.

This same dynamic of increased border enforcement efforts driving flows to the neighboring border sector is found from the other direction as well. In 1997 apprehensions in the easternmost border sector were nearly 244,000; in 2010 they were less than 60,000. In Del Rio the apprehensions in 2000 were 157,000; in 2010 they were less than 15,000. In El Paso in 1993, unlawful crossings were high and apprehensions were more than 285,000. Today, after a significant infusion of resources, they are at only 12,000.

This east-to-west and west-to-east, sector-by-sector reinforcement of the border has funneled flows into the last heavily trekked sector in Tucson. This pincer effect has turned the Tucson sector into ground zero in the border enforcement battle, which, in a bit of law-enforcement hyperbole, senior Border Patrol officials have characterized as the "smugglers' last stand."

Far fewer people are attempting to enter and Border Patrol is interdicting those that do at a far greater rate.

Fewer Apprehensions Means Fewer Attempted Entries

It would be natural to assume that the decrease in apprehensions means that more, not less people are succeeding with their quest to enter the United States. The counterintuitive reality, however, is precisely the opposite. The decrease in apprehensions reflects a dramatic downturn in attempted entries, and, what's more, the *percentage* of individuals apprehended is way up.

It used to be that the number of attempted unlawful entries was simply a "guesstimate" based on the number of apprehensions. In some high-volume places, Border Patrol used to estimate that for every apprehension, two or three attempted entries succeeded. So estimating the number of people who successfully entered was a matter of multiplying apprehensions by a factor of two or three. No longer.

New infrastructure and enhanced technology allows the Border Patrol to know with far more precision how many people attempt to cross the border. By comparing the number of known attempted entries to the number of apprehensions, the agency now has a relatively clear picture of how many individuals actually succeed in crossing unlawfully.

For example, senior Border Patrol officials have advised me that they believe they are apprehending 80-plus percent of the traffic in the still heavily trekked Tucson sector. In other Border Patrol sectors such as El Paso, where the terrain enables deployment of more robust surveillance technology, they believe the percentage of apprehensions is even higher.

In other words, instead of two or three people succeeding every time one person was apprehended, only one person is succeeding for every three or four apprehensions. Far fewer people are attempting to enter and Border Patrol is interdicting [intercepting] those that do at a far greater rate. That adds up to a dramatic decline in successful unlawful border crossings.

The Unintended Consequences of Border Buildup

As set forth above, this strategy of increasing personnel and infrastructure along the border has undeniably succeeded in reducing unlawful entries. But the singular focus on enforcement without complementary legal reforms has triggered a number of unintended and counterproductive consequences.

The ostensible [apparent] goal of this border buildup strategy has been to break the existence of an integrated but unregulated, and therefore illegal, North American labor market. The push and pull of supply and demand, however, are powerful forces. Even with the supply of labor impeded by enforcement and the demand for labor diminished due to the recession, the market has not been destroyed. And attempting to choke off migration without providing alternative legal pathways to channel some level of legitimate economic migration has led to a number of perverse results.

Most importantly, the journey for economic migrants to the United States is far more costly and more perilous than ever before. And the people benefiting from the cost hike are criminal organizations, while those exposed to the perils are migrants who simply want to work or be united with their families and who would prefer to come legally.

The Role of Drug Cartels

As the border has become more difficult to cross—and in the absence of a regulated alternative to unlawful immigration—intending economic migrants have been pushed into the orbit of violent criminal syndicates. Ruthless drug cartels control virtually all illicit cross-border traffic now, including human smuggling.

Because of the increased government control over vast swaths of the border, entry points have moved to more remote and more dangerous junctures. Literally thousands of people have died attempting to cross the border since this buildup began. The average migrant does not know how or where to cross safely, and therefore must find and pay a guide. Virtually all border crossers now require a smuggler.

As noted, these smugglers are not the mom-and-pop operations of yesteryear. The cartels have monopolized the market, subsuming in one way or another all of the extant smuggling operations. As a result, intending migrants are now far more vulnerable than ever. Forced to pay these violent cartels for assistance in crossing, migrants are risking more than ever before. They are forced into more extreme and desperate circumstances. Held for ransom by some smugglers, they are more easily forced to engage in other illegal activity, like muling drugs, or face the prospect of execution or violent reprisals to their families.

It comes as no surprise therefore that what was once a circular flow of economic migrants between the United States and Mexico has been broken. Migrants who make it across the southern border's gauntlet are far less likely to return home (to Mexico or further south) than they once were. The cost and danger of crossing have caused migrants to deepen their roots in this country rather than follow the historical cycle of work and return. In fact, they are so settled that undocumented immigrants are more likely to live with a spouse and children in the United States than U.S. citizens or legal permanent residents are.

Sophisticated New Smuggling Strategies

And as the enforcement presence between the ports of entry has increased, smugglers have devised new strategies for penetrating the border. In some areas, smugglers have developed sophisticated tunneling operations. For example, in Nogales they have made a science of tapping into flood drainage tunnels that run under the border into the United States. Those efforts are being aggressively combated with gates in the tunnels, sensors, and cameras. But they speak to the ingenuity and relentlessness of the smugglers.

With the pressure on the border diminished, it is time to construct an immigration system that preserves the gains in control while disaggregating beneficial migration from the violent drug trade.

Increasingly, smugglers have resorted to pushing cargo (human or contraband) directly through the ports. They pack migrants into trucks and train cars or arm them with increasingly sophisticated fraudulent documentation. This, of course, increases the pressure on inspecting officers to remain vigilant and make smart, quick decisions. While significant funding has gone to Border Patrol to expand their operations between the ports, fewer resources have flowed into Customs and Border Patrol to address the increasing challenges at the ports.

And this pressure on the ports has potentially serious economic consequences. Mexico is our nation's second-largest trading partner but more scrutiny of cross-border traffic means longer wait times, which means less business is getting done. In some cases, trade is deterred altogether. Likewise, Mexican citizens spend billions of dollars ($6.1 billion in FY 2010) each year in the United States. Only citizens of Canada, Japan, and the United Kingdom spend more. Delays in pedestrian and vehicular crossings due to longer border inspections will deter money from being spent in the United States. That hurts U.S. businesses and workers.

In short, the failure to pursue practical legal reforms to our immigration system while deploying this massive surge in enforcement resources has led to unintended, albeit not unsurprising, consequences. With the pressure on the border diminished, it is time to construct an immigration system that preserves the gains in control while disaggregating [separating] beneficial migration from the violent drug trade.

11

Fencing US Borders Will Not Deter Illegal Immigration

Nick Miroff

Nick Miroff is a journalist who covers Mexico, Central America, and the Caribbean and has reported on politics, immigration, crime, and development for The Washington Post.

Although border fences make it more difficult for illegal immigrants to cross the southern border into the United States, they do not prevent them from trying. Since building a fence in the remaining remote areas will be costly, determining the fence's effectiveness is important. In truth, Border Patrol agents claim they cannot watch the fence at all times, and people do climb over and disappear into border cities. Indeed, some analysts suggest that economic and social factors, not fencing, are responsible for the decline in illegal crossings. Although entering the United States illegally remains a challenge, migrant smugglers in Mexico claim there is always a way to get in.

A decade ago, when illegal immigration from Mexico was at an all-time high, this stretch of border [near Calexico, California] was as good a place as any to sneak into the United States.

Migrants and smugglers could slip through the alfalfa fields outside town or plow their pickup trucks through the desert, where the biggest worries were stuck tires and getting safely across the irrigation canals.

An American Great Wall

But in the past five years, the international border here has become a harder, tougher, taller barrier—an American Great Wall. Miles of steel fencing now ride the desolate sand dunes west of Calexico. To the east, giant jack-shaped "Normandy" barriers, named for their resemblance to the defenses that once lined the beaches of northern France in World War II, block off old smuggling routes.

Overall, the United States has added 513 miles of new fencing to its southern boundary since 2006, raising to 649 miles the total length of border that has some form of man-made barrier to people or vehicles. The Rio Grande creates a natural partition along another 1,252 miles, and the government has been putting new fencing there, too.

Now the question is: How much more should be built?

Border Patrol officials say their current plans are to construct just one more mile of fence, in Texas. But as illegal immigration takes an increasingly central role in Republican campaign debates, several GOP candidates have renewed calls to fence the entire 1,969-mile boundary.

President Obama has made light of such proposals, saying fence advocates won't be satisfied until the United States builds "a moat" stocked with "alligators." But leading Republican candidates Mitt Romney and Newt Gingrich have vowed to barricade the entire U.S.-Mexico divide, with Gingrich signing a pledge to install a "double fence" while campaigning in Iowa in early December [2011].

With such an endeavor projected to cost tens of billions of dollars, this stretch of California desert might be as good a place as any to assess how the existing border fence actually works.

The new barriers have been particularly effective at stopping vehicles from coming across, Border Patrol agents say. Along one stretch of desert here, the number of drive-through incursions plunged from 350 in 2007 to four so far in 2011.

But agents also say it is not the case that smugglers and illegal migrants on foot simply go to the place in the desert where the fence ends, and walk around it.

An Ineffective Deterrent

"Anywhere is a good place to sneak across if we're not watching," said Special Agent Jonathan Creiglow, a Border Patrol officer assigned to the agency's El Centro sector here.

Fencing is a tool and a first line of defense, but it does not bestow border security by its mere existence.

But there are also sections of 18-foot fencing right in the middle of downtown Calexico, opposite its sprawling sister city of Mexicali, where border jumpers can be up and over the wall in a matter of seconds, melting into shops and residential streets once they land on the other side.

At night, smugglers toss Hail Marys of pot-stuffed footballs and fling golf-ball-size heroin nuggets over to waiting receivers. Stealthy ultra-light aircraft bomb the lettuce fields outside town with bundles of dope, then swoop back into Mexico, well below radar but high above the fence.

Then there are rugged sections in the desert where fencing is porous or nonexistent, but crossings rare. And those who do try to slip through are tracked by the Border Patrol's growing array of sensors, high-powered night-vision cameras and surveillance drones.

In short, agents say, fencing is a tool and a first line of defense, but it does not bestow border security by its mere existence. "Without the fencing we wouldn't have as much time, but nothing is going to stop them from going over or cutting through it," explained Creiglow, who, at 26, is one of the many recent hires at the Border Patrol, which has doubled in size since 2002, with 18,500 of its 21,500 agents now deployed along the U.S.-Mexico frontier.

A Costly Barrier

Most of the barrier does not sit on the actual international boundary, but slightly north of it, allowing maintenance workers to access both sides without technically crossing into Mexico. Upkeep for the existing 649 miles of fencing is projected to cost $6.5 billion over the next 20 years, according to a 2009 report by the Government Accountability Office, and U.S. Homeland Security officials say the fence was breached 4,037 times in the government's 2010 fiscal year, at an average cost of $1,800 per repair.

With most of the remaining unfenced stretch of border in Texas, the debate has shifted to the question of walling off the Rio Grande. Even in areas where the river can be shallow enough to wade across, putting a fence along the river's sinuous levees is both costly and unpopular with local ranchers who want to preserve riparian access for thirsty cattle.

In Arizona, where Border Patrol agents catch more illegal migrants than anywhere else, lawmakers are soliciting public donations to put barriers along the remaining unfenced 82 miles of the state's 370-mile boundary with Mexico. Such a structure would need to climb up and over steep mountain areas where construction costs are exorbitant and the deterrent value is questionable, enforcement experts say.

"I think the question is: What are you trying to achieve? Just to be able to say that you built a fence on top of a mountain?" said Thad Bingle, who was the Border Patrol's chief of staff from 2007 to 2009. "If someone climbs 10,000 feet to the top of a mountain they aren't going to be deterred by a 10-foot fence."

Construction in rugged areas is made even more pricey because every stretch of new fence needs an accompanying road for maintenance and patrols, he added.

Migrant smugglers on the Mexico side say the fence is hardly their biggest concern.

Fewer Arrests

While the agency tallies the number of migrants it catches, it does not plot the locations of those apprehensions. But after hitting an all-time high of 1.64 million apprehensions in the government's 2000 fiscal year, the number of arrests dropped to 327,577 in the 2011 period which ended Sept. 30, the lowest level since 1972.

Migration experts attribute the decline primarily to the weak U.S. job market—especially the lack of construction jobs—as well as growing fears of kidnapping gangs in northern Mexico. At the same time, average family sizes have fallen dramatically in Mexico, employment opportunities have improved, and the United States is letting more Mexicans in through the front door.

Mexican workers received 516,000 temporary work visas in 2010, "the highest number since the Bracero Program of the late 1950s," said Douglas Massey, an expert on Mexican migration at Princeton University.

Tougher enforcement on the U.S. side has also been a factor, driving up the costs of getting across as well as the difficulty. But migrant smugglers on the Mexico side say the fence is hardly their biggest concern.

"There's too much surveillance now," said Luis, a husky guide-for-hire known as a pollero, standing in the Ninos Heroes park in downtown Mexicali, where recent deportees and would-be border crossers gather. "The Migra [Border Patrol] has cameras everywhere," he said.

Luis wouldn't give his last name, but he said for $500 smugglers will get customers over the fence by creating elaborate diversions for the Border Patrol and deploying teams of helpers with roll-up ladders and ropes, even forming cheerleader-style human pyramids. Better yet, Luis said, for $3,000 a guide will take you over the fence and through the desert at night, and $6,000 buys a legitimate U.S. visa rented from a look-alike with legal status.

"There's always a way in," he said with a wily grin.

12

The Town on the Wrong Side of America's Drugs War

Guy Adams

Guy Adams is a British journalist who was the Los Angeles correspondent for The Independent, *a British newspaper, until 2012.*

In Texas, the border with Mexico is marked by the Rio Grande river. Because the banks of the Rio Grande are prone to flooding and too muddy to build a fence, the metal barrier must cut across US land, marooning some Americans on the wrong side. These Americans claim that the fence has ruined their lives. Not only is the fence ugly, it is also ineffective, as people can easily climb over it if truly motivated. While the border fence may give Americans in other parts of the United States a false sense of security, it disrupts the communities of those who live nearby and leaves Americans unprotected.

Like many a proud Texan, Pamela Taylor likes to mark her turf. So on any given day, she makes sure passers-by can see the Stars and Stripes and the Lone Star Flag of her native state fluttering atop the poles that stand in her front garden.

Ms Taylor has lived in the southern-most city of Brownsville, Texas, since just after the Second World War, when she left the UK [United Kingdom] to join her late husband John, a US soldier who had been based near Birmingham [a city in the UK]. With that in mind, she also flies a Union Jack [the

British flag]. "I hang it lower than the American flags," she says, "because it's a smaller part of my heritage."

Lately, though, there's been a distinctly surreal flavour to Ms Taylor's colourful display of patriotic identity. About 350 metres from her porch, an imposing metal fence looms into view. It is supposed to divide the US from Mexico, but by a cruel twist of fate, the 83-year-old grandmother's family home has ended up on the "wrong" side. Four years ago, amid the seemingly endless hand-wringing over the flow of drugs and illegal migrants across their southern border, Washington politicians voted to erect a tall fence that would stretch thousands of miles from San Diego, on the Pacific coast, to Brownsville, on the Gulf of Mexico. The best-laid political schemes do not always work out as planned, though. When government engineers arrived in Ms Taylor's neighbourhood, their plan hit a snag: the Mexican border follows the meandering Rio Grande in this area. And the river's muddy banks are too soft and too prone to flooding to support a fence.

In total, roughly 50,000 acres of sovereign US land is now on the wrong side of the fence, most of it in Texas.

As a result, this corner of south-eastern Texas had its barrier constructed on a levee that follows a straight line from half a mile to two miles north of the river, leaving Ms Taylor's bungalow—along with the homes and land of dozens of her angry neighbours—marooned on the Mexican side. "My son-in-law likes to say that we live in a gated community," she says, explaining that to even visit the shops she must pass through a gate watched over by border-patrol officers. "We're in a sort of no man's land. I try to laugh, but it's hard: that fence hasn't just spoiled our view, it's spoiled our lives."

Ms Taylor's domestic situation demonstrates—despite sound bites from politicians ([President] Barack Obama last week gave a major speech on the issue)—there are no simple fixes to America's great immigration debate.

In total, roughly 50,000 acres of sovereign US land is now on the wrong side of the fence, most of it in Texas. Lawmakers believe that is a fair price to pay for the political benefits of being seen as "tough" on immigration.

But to many locals, Ms Taylor included, the headline-prone barrier—which cost $7m a mile (£4.3m)—is an expensive white elephant.

"First of all, it doesn't work," she says. "Anyone with a rope and a bucket can just climb on over. Second, they've used it as an excuse to reduce border patrols. Thirdly, it's left people like me unprotected. While the officers are guarding the fence, any drug smugglers can just walk up to my front door."

Like many of her neighbours, Ms Taylor has been forced to turn her home into a mini-fortress, with alarms and motion sensors and a small arsenal of firearms in strategic positions around the house. "We're never safe," she says. "You just try to avoid living in fear."

It was not always like this. For most of the almost 70 years she has lived there, Brownsville has been on the frontline of America's immigration debate. But in the old days, things were less confrontational. Families heading north from Mexico would camp overnight in surrounding cotton fields. "We'd wake up in the morning, and the migrant workers would have built a fire and made tortillas," Ms Taylor says. "On occasion, they'd bring me breakfast."

Ms Taylor once found a woman on her porch in the process of giving birth (she called an ambulance and helped care for the woman until help arrived). Another time, she found an exhausted Hispanic man asleep in her armchair (he apologised, saying he had decided to use her bathroom to shave and brush his teeth).

But from the mid-1990s, with the growth of Mexico's drug trade, security declined. Ms Taylor's car was stolen several times. One morning, she found a package containing 50lbs of marijuana in her flowerbed. "I turned it in to the sheriff," she says. "I'm a cancer patient and when I told my doctor, he said I should have used the stuff."

Since the fence went up, crime has further spiralled. "I'm a gung-ho Texan. I've brought up four kids here and I've made this place my life. But there are times, since the barrier went up, when it hasn't felt like home."

Down the road, she has erected a protest banner. "We're part of America," it says. "We need representation and protection, not a fence."

It made no sense to build this fence, other than making people in other parts of the country feel better and feel a false sense of safety.

You hear a similar sentiment across Brownsville. Roughly eight in every 10 of the city's 170,000 inhabitants are Latino and most speak Spanish as a first language. Every street corner seems to have a taco stall and the local economy relies heavily on imports from factories south of the border.

Most locals rue the divisive tone of the current immigration debate. The city's former mayor, an attorney named Eddie Trevino, who describes himself as a "very right-wing Democrat", says the furore over the fence demonstrates the extent to which the US immigration system needs a complete overhaul.

"Nobody's in favour of illegal immigration," Mr Trevino says. "Let me be unequivocal about that. We don't want anybody violating our laws.

"But the reality is that our laws are antiquated and need to be updated to make sense in the world in which we live. It made no sense to build this fence, other than making people in other parts of the country feel better and feel a false sense of safety. It's like the old joke: build a 12ft fence and you'll be having a huge demand for 15ft ladders."

Even the city's white, Republican-leaning minority is opposed to the border fence. The well-mown greens of a local golf course are on land that now sits on the "wrong" side, while fields and orchards farmed by generations of landowners have been sliced in two by the metal barrier.

"I'll say right off the bat that I'm a conservative—I believe in hard work and I believe our border needs to be secure," says Debbie Loop, whose 15-acre citrus farm is on both sides of the fence. "But when they signed this fence into law, nobody stopped to think Texas isn't Arizona or California. Our border does not run dirt to dirt. Any idiot could have told them that. My grandchildren now live on the wrong side. Who is going to protect them? Who protects me when I'm in my orchards after dusk? I just want to work hard and earn a living. But they've changed this place forever."

This week, Mr Obama signalled his intention to bring the immigration debate into play in next year's [2012] presidential elections, travelling to El Paso, on the other side of Texas from Brownsville, to unveil plans to create a "path to citizenship" for the roughly 12 million undocumented workers thought to be living illegally in the US.

With his speech—aimed to court the growing Latino demographic that now numbers about 50 million people—he entered into electoral-campaign mode. Mr Obama emphasised that his administration has deported more immigrants than that of any of its predecessors. And he ridiculed Republican lawmakers who have endorsed building ever-larger barriers along the border.

"Now they're going to say that we need to quadruple the border patrol," Mr Obama said, reaching out to the large and growing demographic of Latino voters.

"Or they'll want a higher fence. Maybe they'll say we need a moat. Maybe they'll want alligators in the moat. They'll never be satisfied."

The joke might have played well in the next day's news pages—but in Brownsville, they were not laughing.

"Let him come here and say that," was Ms Loop's response.

"Round these parts, people like alligators a whole lot more than politicians."

13

Fenced In

Amy Leinbach Marquis

Amy Leinbach Marquis is associate editor of National Parks, *a publication of the National Parks Conservation Association, an organization that advocates for US national parks and the National Park Service and recommends policies to address threats to the parks.*

The fence along the border between the United States and Mexico, originally designed to prevent illegal immigration in urban areas, now cuts across fragile habitats, posing a threat to migratory wildlife. Sections of the fence now being constructed in Arizona, for example, will disrupt healthy ecosystems for species such as black bears, bighorn sheep, and the jaguar, once considered extinct in the United States. The fence also hinders years of environmental efforts. Moreover, fencing forces illegal immigrants to traverse other fragile habitats, adding to the environmental damage. The destruction of southwest wilderness areas in order to protect national security can be prevented with proper planning.

As America races to secure its Mexican border with 700 miles of double- and triple-layered fencing, wildlife that have never known political boundaries will have no choice but to recognize them now. The fence, originally intended for urban areas, now slices through fragile wildlife habitats that are supposed to be protected by public lands.

Despite sensible arguments that a border fence—no matter how tall, thick, or expensive—won't prevent illegal immigration, Congress voted overwhelmingly for the Secure Fence Act in September 2006, and the Department of Homeland Security is on deadline to finish construction this year. The fence, projected to cost $6 billion, will run piecemeal along the 1,950-mile border from California to Texas.

In Arizona, the fence could pass through private backyards and Indian tribal land, and could obstruct decades of environmental protection on public lands like Cabeza Prieta National Wildlife Refuge, Coronado National Monument, and Organ Pipe Cactus National Monument. These areas offer healthy, intact ecosystems to dozens of imperiled, border-crossing species like the black bear, desert bighorn sheep, Gila monster, and tropical kingbird. Even the federally listed jaguar, considered extinct in the U.S. until 1996, has been making a comeback.

If Congress upholds the Real ID Act, and the fence is built as proposed, there will be a cleansing of species form the borderlands region.

No one denies that these borderlands could benefit from better security. When immigration officials clamp down in urban centers, illegal immigrants funnel into rural areas, damaging fragile habitat and cultural sites. So in one sense, Organ Pipe superintendent Lee Baiza welcomes part of the new 5.2-mile fence near Lukeville, Arizona, a gateway town just south of the park. It could eliminate illegal activity in a historically significant area that has been closed to the public for years because of safety concerns.

But such optimism is generally overshadowed by the fence's impact on park wildlife. Tim Tibbitts, Organ Pipe's wildlife biologist, predicts that coyote, gray fox, and bobcats that travel frequently through this area will be hardest hit. If illegal activity shifts west of the fence, prime Sonoran pronghorn habitat could suffer. "But my biggest concern is that the five miles of fencing we're getting now is just the beginning," he says.

Normally, Organ Pipe would conduct an environmental assessment and public hearing before proceeding with construction, as required by the National Environmental Policy Act. But in the current climate, the Park Service has little say in border decisions; the Real ID Act of 2005 allows Homeland Security to waive legislation that interferes with the construction of physical barriers at the border.

Last year [2007], for example, Homeland Security walled off the San Pedro River Corridor in Arizona without public input or an environmental assessment. When citizen groups successfully sued the agency, Secretary Michael Chertoff used a waiver under the Real ID Act to override the federal judge's ruling and keep building. And in Texas, where the Rio Grande defines the international border, a fence would separate people and wildlife from a critical water source. To encourage compliance, Homeland Security is threatening to sue private landowners, condemn their property, and proceed with construction.

"If Congress upholds the Real ID Act, and the fence is built as proposed[1], there will be a cleansing of species from the borderlands region," says Kim Vacariu, western director for the Wildlands Project in Arizona. Jaguars, he predicts, could disappear first, since so few exist in the U.S. More abundant species like mule deer may decline more slowly, but in time, those populations could become increasingly isolated, and a lack of genetic diversity would make them more prone to disease.

1. The border wall was indeed built across sensitive lands referred to in the article. The Real ID Act, created to improve citizen identification and address other immigration concerns, requires that states standardize driver's licenses or state identity cards to meet federal guidelines. The act remains controversial. On December 20, 2012, the Department of Homeland Security announced that states not in compliance by January 2013 would receive a temporary deferment and that compliance would be revisited in the fall of 2013.

Last year, Defenders of Wildlife produced a report urging Homeland Security to adopt innovative, high-tech cameras and motion sensors that have little to no ecological footprint. The report also suggests partnering with conservation groups and better funding agencies like the Park Service. And last November, NPCA helped Rep. Raúl Grijalva (D-AZ) garner support for the Borderlands Conservation and Security Act, which would give land managers and local communities a say in border security decisions, recognize health and environmental laws, and create a fund to mitigate damage to habitat and wildlife. The bill was sitting idle with the Subcommittee on Border, Maritime, and Global Counterterrorism when the magazine went to print.

"Current immigration and enforcement activities along the border are destroying many of the Southwest's most beautiful wilderness areas, but we don't need to destroy our nation's wildlife, parks, and refuges to protect our national security," says Jamie Rappaport Clark, Executive Vice President of Defenders of Wildlife. "All it takes is a little foresight and planning to protect these important places even as we protect our borders."

14

Fencing US Borders Benefits the Environment

Federation for American Immigration Reform

The Federation for American Immigration Reform (FAIR) is a national, nonprofit organization of concerned citizens who believe in strict immigration policies, increased border security, and limited legal migration.

Environmental groups claim that the massive consumption and waste that accompanies population growth damages the environment. Moreover, as natives and immigrants flee cities for the suburbs, they impact once rural areas. Stabilizing the US population will reduce this environmental degradation. In truth, more than 50 percent of population growth since 1970 has come from immigrants and their children. Clearly, limiting immigration is necessary to slow this growth and in turn protect the environment.

As one of the world's most populous and consumptive nations, the United States has a particular responsibility to control its ecological footprint. To some degree this can be done by moderating our consumer habits or investing in green technology. But lifestyle and technological reforms have not and will not negate the impact of an ever-growing population.

The United States has a population growth rate that is anomalously high among industrialized nations. If there is no change in our growth rate, the U.S. population will increase

40 percent by 2050. Each additional citizen will rightfully demand access to the resources of the nation, the right to consume, and the right to produce waste just as we do. Population stabilization is the key to controlling environmental degradation in the U.S. And the key to population stabilization is immigration reduction.

Establishing Steady State Demographics

Population stabilization means the adoption of a demographic "steady-state" where, over time, the population of the country neither rises nor falls. In such a situation, the average annual population growth rate would be zero. Births and deaths, immigration and emigration would continue to refresh the population and allow it to evolve, but during that process the overall number of people in the country would remain roughly constant.

In a reservoir, the surface of the water naturally fluctuates with the wind and other perturbations, although the level of the water does not rise. Similarly, a stable population would have "surface fluctuations" but would maintain the same size. With a constant stream into and out of a reservoir, it renews itself but does not overflow its capacity. Thus, a stable system is still a dynamic system; a stable population is not stagnant.

> *Limiting immigration is the key to slowing population growth, stabilizing our population, and protecting our environment.*

We cannot achieve such stability overnight. Like any fast-moving object, population growth has an inertia all its own and slowing population growth takes generations. For that reason, it is imperative that we begin now to curb our growth rate, so that we can bequeath a stable population to our descendants. To achieve population stability, we must reduce the current level of immigration. America's native population achieved a "replacement rate" (a birth/death rate where one child is born for each person who dies off—about 2 children per family) in about 1972. Now, over 35 years later, the United States would be well on its way to a stable population were it not for its level of immigration.

Since 1970, our population has grown by about 103 million people. More than half of that growth came from post-1970 immigrants and their descendants. If we do not lower the level of immigration, we will add 132 million people to our population size in the next 40 years—82 percent (106 million) of whom will be post-2005 immigrants and their descendants.

Slowing Population Growth

Because immigration is the driving force behind current population growth in the U.S., limiting immigration is the key to slowing population growth, stabilizing our population, and protecting our environment. Limiting immigration can be accomplished practically and humanely by adhering to the following principles.

- Move from a system of expansive "chain migration" to one of discrete "nuclear family" migration.

- Eliminate the immigration categories for siblings and adult sons/daughters.

- Support an enforceable cap on overall annual immigration of about 300,000.

- Deduct the immediate relatives of an immigrant in the year the primary immigrant enters.

- Admissions under any special, new, or temporary programs (such as amnesties, paroles, or lotteries) should count toward the overall cap, and other admissions should be reduced accordingly.

- Enact a blanket moratorium on future immigration (other than spouses and minor children of U.S. citizens) in order to eliminate the backlog and to get a fresh start.

- Explain these ground rules clearly to the primary immigrant before he/she enters the U.S.

With such changes, the level of immigration would begin to match the level of emigration, and we would develop a 'migration equilibrium' under which immigration would contribute to our economy and society, but not to our population growth. Through reform, immigration can become consistent with our environmental priorities.

The Environmental Impact of Immigration

The environmental pressures caused by immigration-driven population growth are not merely a future possibility; they are a present reality. The daily news teems with tales of the effects of immigration on host communities. Runaway population growth affects not merely the big cities that traditionally receive immigration, but also smaller and more rural communities, which are now receiving both direct immigration and a "secondary migration" of natives fleeing the effects of that population growth. Stories of urban sprawl and the destruction of the surrounding farmland litter the media, and a feeling grows that there is nowhere to run from environmental degradation.

As tempting as it may be to stick our heads in the sand and busy ourselves with less politically sensitive aspects of the problem, we must tackle the immigration aspect as well. Until recently, environmental groups have had little problem either making the connection between immigration and the environment or taking a stance against population growth. In 1965, the year the immigration law was changed to unintentionally generate the current high levels of immigration, the Sierra

Club began asserting the need to limit environmental harm by limiting population growth and immigration. In its 1979 publication Handbook on Population Projections, the Sierra Club noted that "for almost fifteen years, the Sierra Club has acknowledged that population growth is the cause of all environmental problems."

In recent years, however, short-term political fears have begun to silence long-term environmental wisdom. Decision making, even among noted environmental organizations, has been driven more by "political correctness" and a desire to remain insulated from criticism than a fearless devotion to protecting our natural heritage. But the connection between immigration, population, and the environment remains.

15

Fencing the Southern Border of the United States Reflects American Racism

Mark Karlin

Mark Karlin is the editor of BuzzFlash.com, a daily breaking news and commentary website that is a member of the Truthout publishing commnunity. Truthout's goal is to spark public action by revealing injustice and offering a platform for transformative ideas.

The highly militarized fence erected on America's southern border with Mexico demonstrates that racism continues to pervade American politics. The fact that the fence is on the southern border, rather than the northern border with Canada, is telling, since clearly the goal is to keep out people of color. Unsubstantiated claims that immigrants from Mexico and Central America abuse public services and are prone to crime kindle racial anxiety and foster ineffective policies based on fear. Unfortunately, the fence does nothing to prevent the smuggling of drugs or the invasion of US soil by drug cartels. The fence might ease white racial anxiety, but America would be better protected by adopting new policies to combat drug smuggling and address issues of global income inequality.

The physical Mexican-American wall starts as a newly fortified metal barrier extending 300 feet into the warm, balmy waters of Southern California and ends up some 2,000 miles later just east of Brownsville, Texas. But it would be wrong to think of it as continuous, because only about a third of that distance has some form of visible barrier running like a scar across the US border with Mexico.

The origins of the billions of dollars spent on the largely symbolic, highly visible wall really starts much farther north with US organizations and people advocating for a white political power structure, groups like one recently represented at the Conservative Political Action Conference (CPAC), which contend that a multicultural society is a danger to America. The wall also begins with the efforts of states like Arizona to erase Mexican-American culture from the textbooks in state schools, even in districts where the vast majority of students are of Mexican descent. It begins with Republicans such as Mitt Romney welcoming the endorsements of white nationalists who campaign at his side. It starts with draconian Alabama's, Arizona's and Georgia's harsh anti-"immigrant" laws that are spreading to many state legislatures, born of racism and self-serving industry lobbies such as privatized prisons.

The construction of the "barrier" wall—accompanying large-scale militarization (the Border Patrol, Immigration and Customs Enforcement, the FBI [Federal Bureau of Investigation], the Drug Enforcement Agency, the military etc.)—is on America's southern border, and there is meaning in that. Its location is prima facie [apparent] evidence that the "immigration issue" is really a euphemism for keeping poor brown-skinned people out of the US—as well as creating a "practice" zone for protecting American economic and political interests in Mexico and Central America.

Migration Is Not About Opportunism; It's About Survival

The overwhelming majority of migrants from Mexico who seek undocumented entrance to US are desperate, not gold diggers. They are often victims of an indigenous subsistence agricultural and rural economy that is disappearing, due to NAFTA and US subsidies of American farmers, who can sell for lower competitive prices "south of the border." Often facing an arduous, dangerous trip up from southern Mexico or Central America, they are willing to confront possible death in the deserts, sometimes relying on treacherous "coyotes" (guides), who claim to offer them safe passage to the US in return for exorbitant fees, and professional criminals, who abuse and steal from them as they head to the border.

The strong anti-"immigration" laws of many states and the harsh enforcement of the federal government, however, may be backfiring, because migrants in dire economic need will work for very little under squalid conditions—and, therefore, are a valued "commodity." A 2011 *Christian Science Monitor* article notes that in Alabama, "farmers fearing a labor shortage are protesting recent immigration laws they say are too harsh, forcing undocumented workers to flee to prevent deportation." The farmers say, "US workers are unwilling to endure the rigorous conditions of farm work" and that local farmers may go bankrupt. But the proponents of white American exceptionalism have no tolerance for a multicultural society, even if such a stance hurts the US agricultural (and other low-pay labor areas) financial penchant for labor exploitation.

The border wall divides people of common culture and heritage, including not just Mexicans, but also Native Americans.

Can the US Wall Off a Culturally Diverse Society?

"It seems to me that the notion of a literal wall between Mexico and the US signifies both the physical and existential threat that many white Americans perceive from those with darker skin," Timothy Wise, an expert on how the fear of power being shared in America by its diverse population is creating racial anxiety in many whites, told Truthout. "On the one hand, there is the sense that such persons are literally going to harm us—through crime, the mythical overuse of taxpayer funded services or some other thing—and on the other, the larger paranoia that they pose a threat to the cultural and social survival of America as 'we have known it.'"

Recently, I stood in downtown Brownsville on a sliver of land ironically called "Hope Park." I read about how ferries used to cross the narrow stretch of the Rio Grande there, making it easier for the citizens of both nations to move unimpeded from one country to another. Instead, as I looked toward Mexico, there was a high fence of vertical bars in front of me, one of the more "attractive" versions of the wall, which varies in construction design from location to location (in some places it is just corrugated sheets of metal and in others it may be three consecutive physical barriers). "Hope," the celebration of a blended heritage and opportunity, had literally been fenced off from this wedge of land.

The wall is representative of the "genealogy of hate and an entrenched world view which is based upon contempt and disdain for indigenous peoples globally."

The border wall divides people of common culture and heritage, including not just Mexicans, but also Native Americans. Just to the west of Brownsville, is the town of El Calaboz, an indigenous community where Lipan Apache, Tlaxcalteca, Nahua, Comanche and Basque colonists have had extensive interactions since the Spanish colonial era. Margo Tamez, an assistant professor at the University of British Columbia—who holds a cross-appointment in indigenous studies and gender and women's studies—grew up there, learning the history of native oppression from her Lipan Apache elders.

Tamez, like Wise, views the wall as a physical symbol of oppression of peoples who are not white. Talking with Tamez, one gets a sense of the richness of her heritage and what a toll that squashing out diversity—instead of embracing it—takes. Tamez wants her lineage to be clear. She is a member of the Lipan Apache Band of Texas, or in their language, of the Konitsaaíí ndé ("Big Water Clan") and Cúelcahén ("Tall Grass People Clan"), the southernmost of the Athabascan peoples, who stretch from British Columbia to Tamaulipas and Coahuila, Mexico. The Athabascan peoples span three borders, as does their common culture.

Indigenous peoples along the Texas border wall were also the first peoples, according to Tamez, with whom the Spanish colonial government entered into land grants. Tamez's mother, Eloisa García Tamez (whose family was granted a plot in 1767 by Spain), is lead plaintiff in an ongoing lawsuit against the federal government claiming the wall's construction is a violation of Texas land law; Crown land grant and riparian [access to water] laws; treaties among Lipan Apaches, Texas and the US; and international law.

Tamez told Truthout that the wall is representative of the "genealogy of hate and an entrenched worldview which is based upon contempt and disdain for indigenous peoples globally. The wall represents the legacy of that particular world view—a 'deathscape' which is a means of continuing to colonize through mechanization of cages and walls at a vast scale, and which demands its own existence through indigenous peoples' containment in open air prisons in our homelands, our traditional territories." Tamez maintains a web site about the Apache struggle for indigenous rights and lands in which she writes, "Apachean peoples still have a deep sense of being cloistered, imprisoned, contained, detained, and displaced in fractured ways by those visibly militarized architectural features on our territorial spaces."

The Lower Rio Grand Valley
Is a Cage for Many

Indeed, the lower Rio Grand Valley is literally a cage for many. If you travel north by car on the only highway out of Brownsville, Route 77, after about an hour, you come to an immigration checkpoint. If you are undocumented, you will likely be apprehended here and deported, unless you have some foolproof, forged papers. If you are an American citizen (of brown skin color) and are suspected of being an "illegal alien," you may be searched and harassed. In short, without a passport or a driver's license, many residents of the lower Rio Grande Valley are trapped.

Oddly, not only does the wall currently only run along a portion of the border with Mexico, but there are often literally holes (cutouts) in it. Some of the lower Rio Grande Valley residents involved in a losing battle against wall construction say that these gaps prove that its construction is for symbolic political purposes. The Department of Homeland Security (DHS) has countered that there is an "electronic high-tech" wall that covers the cutouts, which were allegedly built so that the ubiquitous white Border Patrol vans, emergency vehicles, farm workers and residents could access the south side of the wall.

Why would people need to access the south side of the wall? Because of a combination of factors—including an international flood plain agreement and political influence that was brought to bear on where the wall was built—there are US residents and agricultural fields south of the wall. Remember that the barricade is supposedly being constructed in order to protect Americans from illegal immigrants and narco trade violence. The people living or working on the "other side" of the wall, if you accept the official version of the intent behind its construction, have been abandoned to marauders.

The Brownsville area home of family farm owner Tim Loop ended up on the south side of the wall, according to an article in *Texas Monthly* (reprinted in *The New York Times*). Loop's horizon view now consists of "imposing sections of 15-to-18-foot-high rust-colored steel bars, some less than 400 feet from Mr. Loop's front porch." But what most concerns Loop is that the DHS has plans to close the "cutouts" in the fence with keypad controlled gates.

"Mr. Loop wonders," *Texas Monthly* writes, "if possessing a secret pass code could make him a target for anyone desperate to gain access to the other side. This is, after all, a familiar area to desperate travelers."

"They tore down hundred-year-old trees to put up a fence," a neighbor of Loop said. "You think they care about how using a keypad is going to affect us?"

Absurdities Do Arise

When a project as large as the wall takes place for reasons of psychological reassurance rather than for its officially stated purpose, absurdities do arise.

One morning, I drove over a humped ridge into the historic Fort Brown Memorial Golf Course, which appeared filled with seniors, all white from what I could see—a scene from a morning retirement community in Florida. Despite University of Texas at Brownsville efforts, the 18-hole course ended up on the south side of the wall—although the barrier was modified in appearance to cross the campus here as a low, chain-link fence with white brick posts and a driveway opening. I drove along what looked like an access road that serviced the links, when in no short time, I turned and saw someone putting up laundry. I was looking over the Rio Grande at Matamoros in Mexico—Brownsville's sister city.

Within a few seconds a Border Patrol van was racing toward me. After reviewing my media credentials and passport, the agent warned me to leave the area because it was "dangerous." I looked to my right and there was a foursome teeing off, just a few yards from the river.

Obviously, it wasn't too dangerous to golf. In fact, on a web site that features golf course reviews, one player at Fort Brown wrote, "this is a very scenic and historical course. It also is a place to enjoy—while you play, native birds and animals [abound]."

The wall gives a false and expensive taxpayer-built sense of easing white racial anxiety.

Yes, there are real issues of jobs being lost in the US, of narco violence and more. But a wall will not stop these problems; the loss of American jobs is primarily due to the shipment of the manufacturing sector to lower-cost countries, and the appetite in the US for illegal drugs will not be halted by a physical barrier. *Time* magazine reports on one of the latest narco evasions of the Mexican border wall (and the vast array of border enforcement strategies), the successful use of submarines manufactured in Colombia for the express purpose of drug transport. A multibillion industry is, like a global corporation, able to financially find a way of getting its product to market.

Easing White Racial Anxiety at What Cost?

According to a 2011 *New York Times* (*NYT*) article, DHS had spent $21 million per mile to build a fence near San Diego (although the costs of construction in Texas are estimated to be lower). Estimates of building a full Mexican border fence range up to $40 billion dollars—and then there are several billion dollars in maintenance costs over the next few years. But Richard Cortez, the mayor of McAllen—just down the road (Route 83) west of Brownsville—told the *NYT*, "It is a winding river [the Rio Grande]. Where in the world are you going to put fencing? To propose that suggests ignorance of the border and the terrain."

Then what is the physical wall, whose continued construction became a big issue early on as part of the "immigration" debate among GOP candidates, for? In some ways, it's a political curtain that's a backdrop for appeasing racial resentment and job losses. It's the way of giving the illusion of an American-gated community for whites. But the wall is also tied into creating a military gateway into neighboring southern countries that need to be "stabilized" for purposes of low-cost labor and open markets. It's just that the wall is a prop, whereas the other law enforcement, intelligence agency and Pentagon initiatives on and around the border are deadly serious.

In that respect, the wall gives a false and expensive taxpayer-built sense of easing white racial anxiety. Complicated, cynical and dangerous cross currents are the real issues swirling along the border, including the lowest-cost labor goals of global corporations, and the hemispheric and narco policies of the United States government.

As Wise observes in his most recent book, *Dear White America: Letter to a New Minority*, "the real problem is less about the distinction between documented and undocumented immigrants, and more about the mere fact of brown-skinned migration in the first place. Many of us simply don't want particular people, no matter the manner in which they come."

Organizations to Contact

The editors have compiled the following list of organizations concerned with the issues debated in this book. The descriptions are derived from materials provided by the organizations. All have publications or information available for interested readers. The list was compiled on the date of publication of the present volume; names, addresses, phone and fax numbers, and email and Internet addresses may change. Be aware that many organizations take several weeks or longer to respond to inquiries, so allow as much time as possible.

American Civil Liberties Union (ACLU)
125 Broad St., 18th Floor, New York, NY 10004
(212) 549-2585
website: www.aclu.org

The American Civil Liberties Union (ACLU) is a national organization that champions the rights found in the Declaration of Independence and the US Constitution. The ACLU Immigrants' Rights Project advocates for the rights of immigrants, refugees, and noncitizens. The Project has published various reports and position papers, including "Mandatory E-Verify: A Giant Plunge into a National ID System," "Beyond the Southwest Border—The CBC Expands the Immigration Debate," and "The U.S.-Mexico Border: Safer than Ever."

American Friends Service Committee (AFSC)
1501 Cherry St., Philadelphia, PA 19102
(215) 241-7000 • fax: (215) 241-7275
e-mail: afscinfo@afsc.org
website: www.afsc.org

The American Friends Service Committee (AFSC) is a Quaker organization that carries out service, social justice, and peace programs throughout the world. An AFSC initiative called Project Voice helps pro-immigrant organizations to lobby for pro-immigrant national immigration policies and immigrants' rights. The AFSC website contains various news updates, brochures, statements, and press releases on illegal immigration, including "Growing Pattern of Border Brutality."

American Immigration Control Foundation (AICF)

PO Box 525, Monterey, VA   24465
(540) 468-2023 • fax: (540) 468-2026
website: www.aicfoundation.com

The American Immigration Control Foundation (AICF) is a lobbying organization that works to influence Congress to adopt legal reforms to reduce US immigration. It supports increased funding for the US Border Patrol, sanctions against employers who hire illegal immigrants, termination of all public assistance except emergency medical for illegal immigrants, and reduction of all immigration. The Foundation vigorously opposes amnesty for illegal immigrants. AICF's website contains news about immigration issues, including those related to securing and closing America's borders.

American Immigration Council

1331 G St. NW, Suite 200, Washington, DC   20005-3141
(202) 507-7500 • fax: (202) 742-5619
website: www.americanimmigrationcouncil.org

The American Immigration Council is a tax-exempt, non-profit educational and charitable organization that works to improve public understanding of immigration law and policy and the value of immigration to American society. Its Immigration Policy Center (IPC) conducts research and analysis about the contributions made to America by immigrants and works to educate and influence the public and policy makers to promote immigrants' rights. The IPC publishes numerous publications on immigration topics, including a blog, *Immigration Impact*, that includes articles on immigration reform such as "High-Skilled Immigration and Entrepreneurship in the Senate's Immigration Bill."

Cato Institute

1000 Massachusetts Ave. NW, Washington, DC 20001-5403
(202) 842-0200 • fax: (202) 842-3490
website: www.cato.org

The Cato Institute is a libertarian public policy research foundation dedicated to stimulating policy debate. It believes immigration is good for the US economy and favors easing immigration restrictions. Its website contains various articles on illegal immigration, including, for example, "Immigrant Myth: Fewer Use Government Services," "Backfire at the Border: Why Enforcement without Legalization," and the video *Using Work Visas to Control the Border.*

Center for Immigration Studies (CIS)

1522 K St. NW, Suite 820, Washington, DC 20005-1202
(202) 466-8185 • fax: (202) 466-8076
e-mail: center@cis.org
website: www.cis.org

The Center for Immigration Studies (CIS) is a conservative, nonprofit think tank devoted to research and analysis of the economic, social, demographic, fiscal, and other impacts of immigration on the United States. The Center generally supports reducing immigration. CIS's website posts background papers, reports, videos, and blogs relevant to the immigration debate. Recent CIS publications include *Legalization vs. Enforcement: What the American People Think on Immigration.*

Federation for American Immigration Reform (FAIR)

25 Massachusetts Ave. NW, Suite 330, Washington, DC 20001
(202) 328-7004 • fax: (202) 387-3447
website: www.fairus.org

The Federation for American Immigration Reform (FAIR) is a national nonprofit, public-interest, and membership organization of concerned citizens dedicated to reforming the nation's immigration policies and slowing or stopping illegal immigration. FAIR seeks to improve border security, to stop illegal immigration, and to reduce annual immigration levels. FAIR's website contains factsheets and publications on the impact of immigration both legal and illegal on the economy, environment, national security, and society. Its recommendations for immigration reform are included in "Seven Principles of True Comprehensive Immigration Reform," available on its website.

The Heritage Foundation
214 Massachusetts Ave. NE, Washington, DC   20002-4999
(202) 546-4400 • fax: (202) 546-8328
website: www.heritage.org

The Heritage Foundation is a public policy research organization that advocates conservative policies based on the principles of individual freedom, free enterprise, limited government, a strong national defense, and traditional American values. The group favors secure borders and strong enforcement of US immigration laws, and it opposes amnesty for illegal immigrants. Its website contains numerous research papers on the subject of illegal immigration. Examples include *Amnesty as an Economic Stimulus: Not the Answer to the Illegal Immigration Problem* and *Help the Economy and Federal Deficit by Raising H-1B Caps.*

Mexican American Legal Defense and Education Fund (MALDEF)
634 S. Spring St., Los Angeles, CA   90014
(213) 629-2512
website: www.maldef.org

The Mexican American Legal Defense and Education Fund (MALDEF) is a nonprofit Latino litigation, advocacy, and educational outreach institution. MALDEF is dedicated to safeguarding the civil rights of US Latinos and empowering the Latino community to fully participate in US society. MALDEF's Immigrants Rights Program seeks to protect the rights of immigrants through litigation and legislative advocacy. Its website lists several publications relevant to immigration, including *Guiding Principles for Comprehensive Immigration Reform.*

The Minutemen Project

Attn: Jim Gilchrist, PO Box 3944
Laguna Hills, CA   92654-3944
(949) 587-5199
e-mail: JimGilchrist@MinutemanProject.com
website: www.minutemanproject.com

Founded by immigration activist Jim Gilchrist in 2004, the Minuteman Project is a grassroots volunteer organization with local chapters that advocate enforcement of US immigration laws and halting illegal immigration. The group's website contains press releases, blogs, and other information about its activities. Recent publications include *California: Mexico's Maternity Ward* and *U.S. Taxpayer Funding Education of Mexican Children.*

National Council of La Raza (NCLR)

1126 16th St. NW, Suite 600, Washington, DC   20036
(202) 785-1670 • fax: (202) 776-1792
e-mail: comments@nclr.org
website: www.nclr.org

The National Council of La Raza (NCLR) is a national Hispanic civil rights and advocacy organization that works to improve opportunities for Hispanic Americans. NCLR conducts research, policy analysis, and advocacy to provide a Latino perspective in five key areas: assets/investments, education, employment and economic status, health, and civil rights/ immigration. The organization recognizes the right of the United States to control its borders and supports measures that would strengthen border enforcement so long as such enforcement is conducted fairly, humanely, and in a nondiscriminatory fashion. NCLR's website includes analysis of immigration legislation and various publications relevant to the border security debate. Some examples include *Five Facts About Undocumented Workers in the United States.*

National Immigration Forum

50 F St. NW, Suite 300, Washington, DC 20001
(202) 347-0040 • fax: (202) 347-0058
website: www.immigrationforum.org

The National Immigration Forum is an immigrant rights organization dedicated to promoting public policies that welcome immigrants and refugees. It advocates for open-border immigration policies that are supportive of newcomers to the United States. The Forum's website contains press releases, a blog, and other publications, such as "What Does Smart and Effective Border Security Look Like?" and "The 'Border Bubble': A Look at Spending on U.S. Borders."

National Network for Immigrant and Refugee Rights (NNIRR)

310 Eighth St., Suite 303, Oakland, CA 94607
(510) 465-1984 • fax: (510) 465-1885
e-mail: nnirr@nnirr.org
website: www.nnirr.org

The National Network for Immigrant and Refugee Rights (NNIRR) is a national organization composed of local coalitions and immigrant, refugee, community, religious, civil rights, and labor organizations and activists. It seeks to educate the public about immigration issues and it promotes US immigration policies that protect the rights of all immigrants and refugees, regardless of immigration status. Recent publications include *Over-Raided, Under Siege: US Immigration Laws and Enforcement Destroy the Rights of Immigrants.*

NumbersUSA

1601 N Kent St., Suite 1100, Arlington, VA 22209
(703) 816-8820
website: www.numbersusa.com

NumbersUSA is a nonprofit, nonpartisan, public policy organization that opposes high levels of immigration and seeks to educate the public about immigration numbers and the recommendations on immigration from two national commissions of the 1990s. The group's website features a blog and numerous articles about illegal immigration and other immigration issues. Recent publications include the book *The Case Against Immigration* and the article "With Jobless Rates Like These, How Can Anybody Consider More Foreign Workers or an Amnesty?"

Pew Hispanic Center

1615 L St. NW, Suite 700, Washington, DC   20036-5610
(202) 419-3600 • fax: (202) 419-3608
e-mail: info@pewhispanic.org
website: www.pewhispanic.org

The Pew Hispanic Center is a nonpartisan research organization whose mission is to improve understanding of the US Hispanic population and chronicle Latinos' growing impact on the nation. The Center does not take positions on policy issues, but it has published numerous reports and research studies on immigration issues, including the reports *A Nation of Immigrants* and *A Portrait of Unauthorized Immigrants in the United States.*

United States Conference of Catholic Bishops (USCCB)

3211 Fourth St. NE, Washington, DC   20017
(202) 541-3000
website: www.usccb.org

The United States Conference of Catholic Bishops (USCCB) is an assembly of Catholic bishops who work to unify, coordinate, promote, and carry on Catholic activities in the United States. One of the group's priorities is helping immigrants, and the USCCB advocates for amnesty to legalize the millions of illegal immigrants living in the United States. Its website provides information about immigration issues, including publications such as the position paper "The Catholic Church's Teaching on Immigration Enforcement" and the assembly address "The Immigration Experience at the Border."

U.S. Citizenship and Immigration Services (USCIS)

20 Massachusetts Ave. NW, Washington, DC   20529
(800) 375-5283
website: www.uscis.gov

The U.S. Citizenship and Immigration Services (USCIS) is a part of the Department of Homeland Security (DHS). USCIS replaced the former U.S. Immigration and Naturalization Service (INS), which was abolished on March 1, 2003, and it is charged with processing immigrant visa petitions and providing other immigration services. The USCIS website contains links to other immigration enforcement entities, including the U.S. Immigration and Customs Enforcement (ICE) and the U.S. Customs and Border Protection (CBP).

Bibliography

Books

Edward Alden

The Closing of the American Border: Terrorism, Immigration, and Security Since 9/11. New York: Harper Perennial, 2009.

George Andreopoulos, ed.

Policing Across Borders: Law Enforcement Networks and the Challenges of Crime Control. New York: Springer, 2013.

Kathleen R. Arnold

American Immigration After 1996: The Shifting Ground of Political Inclusion. University Park, PA: Pennsylvania State University Press, 2011.

Jagdish Bhagwati and Gordon Hanson, eds.

Skilled Immigration Today: Prospects, Problems, and Policies. New York: Oxford University Press, 2009.

Barry R. Chiswick, ed.

High-skilled Immigration in a Global Labor Market. Washington, DC: AEI Press, 2011.

Michael Dear

Why Walls Won't Work: Repairing the US-Mexico Divide. New York: Oxford University Press, 2013.

D. Robert DeChaine, ed.

Border Rhetorics: Citizenship and Identity on the US-Mexico Frontier. Tuscaloosa, AL: University of Alabama Press, 2012.

Natasha T. Duncan — *Immigration Policymaking in the Global Era: In Pursuit of Global Talent.* New York: Palgrave Macmillan, 2012.

Cari Lee Skogberg Eastman — *Shaping the Immigration Debate: Contending Civil Societies on the US-Mexico Border.* Boulder, CO: First Forum Press, 2012.

Kevin R. Johnson and Bernard Trujillo — *Immigration Law and the US-Mexico Border: ¿Si Se Puede?* Tucson, AZ: University of Arizona Press, 2011.

Steven G. Koven and Frank Goetzke — *American Immigration Policy: Confronting the Nation's Challenges.* New York: Springer, 2010.

Mark Krikorian — *The New Case Against Immigration: Both Legal and Illegal.* New York: Sentinel, 2008.

Robert Lee Maril — *The Fence: National Security, Public Safety, and Illegal Immigration Along the US-Mexico Border.* Lubbock, TX: Texas Tech University Press, 2011.

Ryan Pevnick — *Immigration and the Constraints of Justice: Between Open Borders and Absolute Sovereignty.* New York: Cambridge University Press, 2011.

Christopher Heath Wellman and Phillip Cole — *Debating the Ethics of Immigration: Is There a Right to Exclude?* Oxford, UK: Oxford University Press, 2011.

Periodicals and Internet Sources

Edward Alden and Bryan Roberts	"Are U.S. Borders Secure?" *Foreign Affairs*, July/August 2011.
Greg Beato	"Big Brother's Border Blindness: After 15 Years and Hundreds of Billions of Dollars, the Virtual Border Fence Is Still Just a Mirage," *Reason*, December 2012.
Bryan Caplan	"Why Should We Restrict Immigration?" *Cato Journal*, Winter 2012.
Charles S. Clark	"Immigration Debate," *CQ Researcher Update*, December 10, 2010.
Frank Clifford	"The Border Effect," *American Prospect*, September 18, 2012.
Susan Crabtree	"Graham Calls Immigration Reform Dead if U.S. Borders Aren't Secured," *The Hill*, April 28, 2010.
Michael Cutler	"Terrorists Are Among the Vast Majority of Illegals," NewsWithViews.com, March 3, 2009. www.newswithviews.com.
Lyle Denniston	"Constitution Check: Can a State Close Its Borders Entirely to Undocumented Immigrants?" *Huffington Post*, May 1, 2012. www.huffingtonpost.com.

Federation for American Immigration Reform — "Immigration, Poverty and Low-Wage Earners: The Harmful Effects of Unskilled Immigrants on American Workers," 2011. www.fairus.org.

Aaron D. Flesch et al. — "Potential Effects of the United States-Mexico Border Fence on Wildlife," *Conservation Biology*, 2009.

Julie Grant — "U.S.-Canadian Border Changes Since 9/11," North Country Public Radio, September 9, 2011. www.northcountrypublicradio.org.

Daniel Griswold — "Higher Immigration, Lower Crime," *Commentary*, December 2009.

Susan W. Hardwick and Adriana E. Martinez — "Building Fences: Undocumented Immigration and Identity in a Small Border Town," *Focus on Geography*, Winter 2009.

David T. Jones — "Open Borders and Closing Threats," *International Journal*, Spring 2012.

Kenneth Jost — "Immigration Conflict," *CQ Researcher*, March 9, 2012.

Reed Karaim — "America's Border Fence," *CQ Researcher*, September 19, 2008.

Melanie Mason — "The Border Fence Folly," *New Republic*, June 30, 2008.

Michael A. Meighen — "FDR's Advice for Managing the U.S.-Canadian Border Resonates Today," *Seattle Times*, August 17, 2011.

Edwin Mora   "Canadian Border Bigger Terror Threat than Mexican Border, Says Border Patrol Chief," *CNS News*, May 18, 2011. www.cnsnews.com.

Johanna Neuman   "Swine Flu: Time to Close the U.S.-Mexico Border?" *Los Angeles Times*, April 28, 2009.

Alex Newman   "Feds Purposely Keeping U.S. Borders Wide Open, Experts Say," *New American*, February 20, 2012.

Scott Nicol   "Costly Fence on US-Mexico Border Is Effective—Only in Hurting Nature," *Christian Science Monitor*, February 27, 2011.

Alex Nowrasteh   "The Economic Case Against Arizona's Immigration Laws," *Policy Analysis*, September 25, 2012. www.cato.org.

Robert J. Sampson   "Rethinking Crime and Immigration," *Contexts*, Winter 2008.

Christopher Sherman   "U.S. and Mexico Disagree Over Border Fence," *Huffington Post*, July 24, 2012. www.huffingtonpost.com.

Steven L. Taylor   "The Ongoing Insanity of US Border Policy," *Outside the Beltway*, September 29, 2011.

U.S. News & World Report   "Should the United States Build a Fence on Its Southern Border?" October 25, 2011.

Roger Waldinger   "Immigration: The New American
                   Dilemma," *Daedalus*, Spring 2011.

Index